M000224247

Reaches of Empire

The Social Foundations of Aesthetic Forms Series
Jonathan Arac, Editor

The Social Foundations of Aesthetic Forms
A series of
COLUMBIA UNIVERSITY PRESS
Jonathan Arac, Editor

*Critical Genealogies: Historical Situations for
Postmodern Literary Studies*
Jonathan Arac

*Advertising Fictions: Literature, Advertisement,
and Social Reading*
Jennifer Wicke

Masks of Conquest: Literary Study and British Rule in India
Gauri Viswanathan

Left Politics and the Literary Profession
Lennard J. Davis and M. Bella Mirabella, eds.

The Vietnam War and American Culture
John Carlos Rowe and Rick Berg, eds.

*Authors and Authority: English and American
Criticism, 1750–1990*
Patrick Parrinder

REACHES
OF
EMPIRE

The English Novel
from Edgeworth to Dickens

Suvendrini Perera

COLUMBIA UNIVERSITY PRESS
NEW YORK

Columbia University Press
New York   Oxford

Copyright © 1991 Columbia University Press
All rights reserved

Library of Congress Cataloging-in-Publication Data

Perera, Suvendrini.
    Reaches of empire : the English novel from Edgeworth to Dickens /
Suvendrini Perera.
        p.   cm.—(The Social foundations of aesthetic forms)
    Includes bibliographical references and index.
    ISBN 0–231–07578-2 (alk. paper)
    1. English fiction—19th century—History and criticism.
    2. Imperialism in literature.   3. Colonies in literature.
    I. Title.   II. Series: Social foundations of aesthetic forms series.
PR868.I54P47   1991   91–22769
823'.809358—dc20   CIP

"Don't talk to me about Matisse," by Lakdasa Wikkramasinha, quoted by kind per-
mission of Tisara Prakasakayo, Dehiwala, Sri Lanka.

An early version of chapter 3 was first published in *Victorian Studies,*
volume 33, no. 4 (Summer 1990).

Casebound editions of Columbia University Press
books are Smyth-sewn and printed on permanent and
durable acid-free paper.
Printed in the United States of America
                    c 10 9 8 7 6 5 4 3 2 1
                    p 10 9 8 7 6 5 4 3 2 1

For my mother,
Leila Kanagasabai,
with whom I first read nineteenth-century novels
high in the up-country of Sri Lanka
and for
Mahinda Perera
who emboldened me to test that reading

❦

Contents

Preface ix

Acknowledgments xi

Introduction: Reading Noncollusively 1

1 • *Interruption, Interpolation, "Improvement":*
Inscribing Abolition and "Amalgamation"
in Edgeworth's Belinda 15

2 • *Proper Places: Spatial Economies in Austen and*
Gaskell 35

3 • *"Wholesale, Retail, and for Exportation": Empire*
and the Family Business in Dombey and Son 59

4 • *"Fit Only for a Seraglio": The Discourse of Oriental*
Misogyny in Jane Eyre *and* Vanity Fair 79

5 • *"All the Girls Say Serve Him Right": The Multiple*
Anxieties of Edwin Drood 103

Conclusion 123

Notes 127

References 147

Index 161

❧

Preface

$\mathcal{L}$*EONARD WOOLF'S Growing,* an autobiography of his years
as a colonial administrator, frequently refers to the author's sense
of living a literary construct. To make sense of and in turn represent "the crude exoticism of what was to be my life or my dream
for the next few years" (1961:22), Woolf relies on the authority of
literature, most often on the tradition of the English novel. "I
could never make up my mind," he remarks early on, "whether
Kipling had moulded his characters accurately in the image of
Anglo-Indian society or whether we were moulding our characters
accurately in the image of a Kipling story" (46).[1] And Kipling,
though the most obvious of Woolf's sources, is not the only one.
Woolf's experience as a self-proclaimed "imperialist" in the country then known as Ceylon—his difficult interactions with the anglicized lawyers of Jaffna and the Sinhala peasants of Hambantota;
his awkward semicourtship of two young Englishwomen, Rachel
and Gwen; his sexual encounter with an anonymous Sri Lankan
"loose liver" on a sultry Jaffna evening—all are mediated through
literary originals from Austen to Conrad.

"Indeed," as Rachel Blau DuPlessis maintains, "narrative may
function on a small scale the way that ideology functions on a large
scale—as 'a system of representations by which we imagine the

world as it is' " (1985:3). This book is a study of empire and the great tradition of the English novel; more specifically, of the ways in which empire is imaginatively constituted and constructed within the mainstream of the English novel.

My objective is twofold in reading a tradition often seen as insular and insulated within the unfamiliar cultural context of empire: I hope not only to relocate or recontextualize the novel form itself but to suggest that such a revision might lead in turn to a fuller understanding of the literary constitution of empire. Such revision, of course, becomes immediately relevant in the context of the arguments now being waged in educational institutions both in the United States and elsewhere over the role of "great books" and the need for "a curriculum of inclusion."[2] As Rosemary Hennessy and Rajeswari Mohan write in a carefully detailed essay outlining what they name a "global reading strategy": "history is never accessible outside its production through reading in and for the ideological problems posed in the present. In this sense, *reading is a material practice contributing to the construction of the social real; any reading of any text of culture is first of all an intervention in the available ways of making sense of 'history' in the subject's historical present*" (1989:326; emphasis added). The purpose of a historically conscious reading is not to illuminate or restore a "lost" past to the key narratives I study but to identify and examine the role of those past narratives in ordering our present.

This book reads the great cultural texts of English literature as they work to construct empire at the primary levels of vocabulary, image, character, place, plot, narrative—levels whose currency in the "post" or neocolonial world depends almost entirely on their invisibility or "natural" accessibility. Although these texts do not confront imperial experience directly, their power is that they constitute that experience at (and for) the center, a largely undetected process that shapes more immediate representations of empire in later periods and other forms of discourse.

Finally, in examining these key narratives by Austen, Charlotte Brontë, Dickens, Edgeworth, Gaskell, Thackeray, and others, I hope to suggest a strategy for reading empire in narratives that have been perceived as indifferent to or distanced from imperial ideology—a strategy by no means intended to be limited to the individual texts and authors I discuss.

Acknowledgments

*T*HIS BOOK is the product of living and reading on three continents, but it was written mostly in New York City, originally as a doctoral dissertation submitted to the English Department at Columbia University. During those years it was my privilege to work with two dissertation sponsors who not only heartened by their ready appreciation and understanding but inspired by their own exemplary critical practice. It gives me great pleasure to record here my thanks to Edward Said for his staunch and generous support and to Carolyn Heilbrun for her constant interest and friendship.

My colleagues at Columbia, Lisa Gittelman, Beth Harrison, Susan Heath, Jon Smith, and Julie Abraham each read one or more chapters of the dissertation at various stages of its development. I thank them for their attentive critiques. I am also grateful to Professor Barbara Fields of the History Department at Columbia, Professor Patrick Brantlinger of the English Department at Indiana University, and an anonymous reviewer for Columbia University Press for their insightful comments on the original dissertation.

The genealogy of this book, I have already said, goes beyond my years at Columbia; it also includes a number of wonderful teachers and friends. Among them I want to name especially Nalini MacIntyre from my schooldays in Colombo and the late Doric de Souza and the late Ranjit Goonewardene at the University of Sri Lanka. At Washington University, I am grateful to Steven Zwicker for first encouraging me to think systematically about "literature and history" (and for seeing I got paid for it) and to Naomi Lebowitz, unfailing mentor and friend.

Finally, my most profound obligation is to Mahinda Perera, whose contribution throughout this project has been incalculable. *Reaches of Empire* represents, among other things, one more discovery we have made together over the years.

❧

Introduction: Reading Noncollusively

> *It is because there is so much novels cannot possibly know that they know what they do, and in the form they do.*
>
> . . . . . .
>
> *Criticism['s] . . . task is not to redouble the text's self-understanding, to collude with its object in a conspiracy of eloquence. Its task is to show the text as it cannot know itself, to manifest those conditions of its making (inscribed in its very letter) about which it is necessarily silent.*
>
> — *TERRY EAGLETON,*
> CRITICISM AND IDEOLOGY

*T*HE BRITISH Empire, long invisible in literary studies, is beginning to materialize in the work of recent critics as the success of that particular imperialist project recedes. With one or two recent exceptions, such work has focused mainly on literature produced during and after the last three decades of the nineteenth century.[1] From the 1870s on, empire is indeed an inescapable, even obsessive theme in literature, in the work of novelists of a range of interests and backgrounds—from Schreiner, Kipling, Conrad, and Forster to Haggard, Conan Doyle, and Henty. Following J. R. Seeley's famous pronouncement in 1883 that England "had conquered and peopled half the world in a fit of absence of mind" (1972:12), these novels have been considered characteristic of a period when England roused itself from a state of delightful amnesia about empire to a consciousness of imperial responsibility.

The notion of an *Age of Empire* emerging in the last decades of the century, however, obscures the extent of England's imperial involvement up to this point. This study argues that imperial ideology, far from being an incidental intrusion of the late Victorian period, was throughout a major factor in the English novel and had, in fact, a crucial, shaping role in the development of the form itself. *Reaches of Empire* examines the ways in which the major practitioners of the English novel from Edgeworth to Dickens produced empire during the first seventy years of the nineteenth century, a period when both novel and empire made some of their most significant advances.

ॐ

In *The Mythology of Imperialism,* a study of "novelists of empire" from Kipling to Joyce Cary, Jonah Raskin writes of the early decades of the nineteenth century:

> In daily life the fact of empire was difficult to forget. Yet the Victorian novelists imagined that the colonies were peripheral to their domestic concerns, and rarely felt that the colonial world impinged on the metropolis. In Victorian novels the colonies are usually places to transfer burned out characters, or from which to retrieve characters. . . . They are especially convenient for the beginnings, turning points and endings of fiction. The plot began— or flagging interest was revived—when a character returned from abroad, and the action terminated when the characters left for the colonies. For the Victorians existence meant existence in England: it began when they returned to Southampton or Liverpool and it ended when they embarked for Australia, Canada or Nigeria. Going to India was like falling off a cliff. The Englishman coming back to London felt like a fish thrown back into the sea after flopping about on land. (1971:17–18)

In this remarkable passage, Raskin at once brilliantly outlines and dismisses the ways in which empire functions in the economy of early and mid–nineteenth-century novels: it is peripheral, a space "off" where characters await their cues to appear in the action, yet at the same time "especially convenient for the beginnings, turning points and endings of fiction"—that is, the source of action.

This study examines the function of empire in the early and mid–nineteenth-century novel precisely because its peripheral presence there seems suggestive and significant. Implicit in Raskin's imagery of metropolis and hinterland is the production of political and cultural definition; by designating center and mar-

gins, charting the limits of alien and native elements, inimical land
and life-giving sea, the novel maps the boundaries between self
and other, grounding each in specifically constituted locations.
The project of *Reaches of Empire* is to read those peripheral spaces
as they appear at the edges of early and mid–nineteenth-century
texts, and to attend to what is unsaid and occluded in them. For if
to go to India is to fall off a cliff, the absence over the other side is
itself telling: not blank but a space accessible to reading. To name
its colonized periphery a blank is precisely the function of imperial
discourse. Carlyle's pronouncement that "the West India Islands
. . . till the white European first saw them . . . were as if not yet
created . . . lying all asleep, waiting the white enchanter" (1849:674–
75) is an instance of this discursive strategy; as is Conrad's "Africa,"
an alluring blank on a map, inviting the cartographer's exploratory
pencil.[2] In insisting that the unrepresented space over the side of
the cliff is a site of inscription, *can* be read, the critic challenges
and refuses the silence so crucial to that strategy's success.

Belonging over the side of the cliff and generated out of that
absence is the machinery of Raskin's "beginnings, turning points
and endings." These elements—voyages, transportations, migrations; magical appearances and disappearances of goods and capital; a cast of exotic Others that includes servants, heiresses, and
rogues—are in their plenitude the characteristic stuff of fiction,
the material that constitutes the form in the period I discuss. They,
too, are read in the following chapters; not as extraneous props or
"plot devices" (as they are generally seen) but as productions of
the defining oppositions between center and margins, generated
in their multiple manifestations from a specific imperial history.
As such, they contribute in turn to that ongoing discourse through
which empire was constituted, managed, and contested throughout the nineteenth century.

To connect the formal and textual characteristics of the novel
with empire might be a departure in some ways; previous studies
of the relationship between literature and empire have tended to
examine works linked by thematic or geographical rather than
primarily generic factors. For example, Patrick Brantlinger draws
on histories, travel narratives, and adventure tales as well as novels
in his *Rule of Darkness* (1988), a survey of imperial themes and
tropes in Victorian literature. Similarly, Peter Hulme's *Colonial
Encounters* (1986) uses a range of texts (including Columbus' *Journal*, *Robinson Crusoe*, and *The Tempest*) to dissect "moments in a

developing discourse which was attempting, in a variety of ways, to manage Europe's understanding of its colonial relationships with native Caribbean societies" (2). These works, together with the contributions of Edward Said, Gayatri Spivak, Homi Bhabha, V. G. Kiernan, Martin Bernal, Gauri Viswanathan and others, have been important in establishing the role of imperial ideology in a range of literary discourses. I hope, by concentrating on the mainstream novel in this study, both to emphasize that the "man-age[ment] of Europe's understanding of its colonial relationships" extends beyond writing that directly confronts imperial situations and to posit a particular relation between that form and empire. For the most part, the novels chosen are of the metropolis and distinctly insular in setting, although empire exists, as noted earlier, on their margins. With the possible exception of Edgeworth (whose inclusion will become self-explanatory in chapter 1), the novels read here are by major, "canonized" authors; taken together, they represent the central literary tradition of the nineteenth century.

In his 1979 *Dreams of Adventure, Deeds of Empire,* Martin Green puts forward an interesting analogy between the impact of workers' institutes on literary studies at the beginning of the twentieth century and the growing influence of immigrants from former colonies at its close. Then,

> people studying literature found in the great eighteenth- and nineteenth-century novels moral discriminations and literary achievements that invited explanation in terms of the class system and the Industrial Revolution. Those novels told the story of the sisters and their courtship. But critics and scholars . . . found a way to give them a commentary which led naturally into political truths, without ceasing to be literary criticism. . . . The classics of English literature were set before the working class reader, and both books and readers were tested and extended, each by the challenge of the other. . . . Nowadays, I think the innocent and disinherited are not working class but immigrant. *They* are the people of England; theirs are the hands we see reaching up in the public libraries for the big volumes so strange to them, so familiar to us. (xiv–xv)

But if for Green immigrant or postcolonial readers have replaced the indigenous working class as aspiring interpreters of "the big volumes" of English culture, he identifies their key texts as very different: "It was the Great Tradition novels which could be explained in terms of class conflict and industrialization. It is the adventure novels which could be explained in terms of empire; and which could . . . bring together native population and immigrants, if they were properly studied" (xv). Green's book is an admirable, principled attempt to accomplish this reconciliation by undertaking a serious reappraisal of the "adventure novel" from Defoe to Conrad.[3] In doing so, he endorses two separate and unequal traditions of fiction: the less "serious" romance or adventure genre, which is expansionist in ideology, explores territories outside the metropolis (Crusoe's island, Scott's premodern Highlands, Fenimore Cooper's western frontier), and is primarily a story of "brothers" and male bonding; and second, the "serious" and prestigious "Great Tradition," a story of "sisters and their courtship," which focuses on the domestic and English and is always implicitly, and often explicitly, anti-imperialist in ideology (1979:56–65).

My focus in this book is precisely the set of "big volumes" that, for Green (and others), are largely irrelevant to the concerns of empire, both because they were domestic narratives about "sisters" and marriage, and because they either criticized crude expansionism or loftily "ignored" it. Green is not the only critic to accept antiwar or antiexpansionist sentiments in the novel at face value; however, the set of ideas and perceptions around empire is often more complicated and contradictory than such a distinction implies.[4] Overt opposition to expansionism does not necessarily imply opposition to empire itself, much less the absence of imperial ideology. Before dealing with Green's related categorization of the novel by gender, I will briefly examine the distinction he proposes between the "serious" and "adventure" categories of fiction.[5]

In English history, the enmeshing of literature and empire can be traced at least as far back as Spenser's prescriptions for a recently colonized Ireland.[6] From then on, English literature expanded simultaneously with England's empire, not in simple correspondence but in a complex and symbiotic relationship. In the case of the novel, Said has noted a "far from accidental convergence between the patterns of narrative authority constitutive of the novel on the one hand, and on the other, a complex ideological configuration underlying the tendency towards imperialism" (forthcoming). This entwined relationship may be seen as early as 1688 in one of the first novels in English, Aphra Behn's *Oroonoko*, a tale of slave uprising in colonial Surinam. About thirty years later, *Robinson Crusoe*, nominated by critical tradition as the proto-typical modern novel, suggests the complex relation between the newly expanding systems of capitalism and colonial domination.[7] So, to a lesser degree, does Defoe's less popular *Life, Adventures and Piracies of the Famous Captain Singleton* (1720), the narrative of an English pirate who prospects for gold in Africa, trades slaves in North America and spices in the Indian Ocean, then returns to settle in England, a repentant but enormously wealthy man.

In Green's analysis, a split occurs at this point between the external, adventurous interests of Defoe and the novel of domestic and psychological interest developed by Richardson and Fielding in the 1740s. But the distinction between "internal" and "external" or "domestic" and "adventurous" is by no means absolute: Crusoe, Moll Flanders, and the Quaker William in *Captain Singleton* are subjects of considerable internal, "psychological" interest, while *Pamela* and *Tom Jones* actively participate in the discourses of mobility, advancement, and expansion at the heart of Defoe's work.[8] Similarly, despite their domestic settings, the early epistolary novels of Richardson and Burney were, like the works of Defoe and Swift, based on a dynamic of center and margins, a "to and fro" connection between action and narrative. Again, throughout this period, "Oriental Tales" were part of the regular output of literary figures like Goldsmith, Addison, and Steele as well as of novelists like Sterne and Smollett. Johnson's *Rasselas, Prince of Abyssinia* (1759) is the best-known example of this genre, though Martha Conant's 1908 study, *The Oriental Tale in England*, lists hundreds of other instances.[9] The spate of "national" and Gothic novels early in the nineteenth century (including those of Scott and his ac-knowledged model, Edgeworth) also challenges any simple distinc-tion between "domestic" novelists and the novelists of external, nonmetropolitan territories.

The connection between the development of the novel and of empire in the nineteenth century was noted early on by Susanne Howe in her 1949 *Novels of Empire* (though the body of her book deals with a later era and the novels she examines are those with colonial settings). Howe's introductory remarks link the expanding boundaries of empire with the simultaneous burgeoning of the novel form:

The Expansion of England worked its way naturally into the Victo-rian novel. At first this new theme was absorbed genially, uncriti-cally, into that capacious embrace. In the happy fifties and somewhat less happy sixties . . . the novel was sprouting and leafing out with a kind of Elizabethan exuberance into the most prodigious of the literary forms. Hardly anybody noticed the stories and the people of a greater and greater Britain mingling in its rich and cheerful confusion. Yet they were there, the innocent heralds of dark days to come. . . . From the thirties to the seventies, fiction began slowly to trundle in the footsteps of colonial expansion. (3)

In her analogy between empire and the "most prodigious of literary forms," Howe comes close to suggesting a causal relationship between that most characteristic literary form of high Victorianism, the triple-decker novel, and the acquisition and incorporation of "greater Britain." But if she is one of the first critics to recognize the impact of imperial ideology on the Victorian novel, the passage also suggests that Howe is less aware of the novel's implication in the production of that ideology. For Howe, the novel itself is only a natural and innocent medium ("sprouting and leafing," "absorbed genially, uncritically," "rich and cheerful confusion"). Her perception of literature's role in empire is aptly summed up in her image of Fiction, clumsy, unsuspecting, well-intentioned, "trundl[ing] in the footsteps of colonial expansion."

Later critics (Foucault, Macherey, Said) have shown the relation between the novel and ideology in a context that no longer accommodates this innocent personification. Empire is not simply expressed or reflected in the novel; in the period I discuss, it is rather processed and naturalized by it. This is not to suggest that the novel "caused" or was responsible for empire but that certain fictional practices—the ordering of empire in fiction—prepared for, or made possible a climate for receiving or accommodating, empire. "The novel follows the flag," Howe claims later in the same passage; but it also advances before it, producing conditions for the flag's reception through which empire also can be read retrospectively, in a variety of ways.[10] To make the point a little differently, it is not only that the novel would be a different form without empire but that empire is unimaginable in its particular form without its processing and legitimation in the novel. The detail of this activity of processing is, ultimately, the subject of this book.

❧

The management of empire in the novel, I have already suggested, occurs not only, or even chiefly, in narratives that deal directly with colonized territories. The representation of empire draws on a preexisting and continually expanding vocabulary for confronting and regulating other forms of cultural domination. George Stocking points out, for example, that the language of class difference provided an easily accessible model for the representation of imperial relationships: "There was . . . a close articulation, both experiential and ideological, between the domestic and the colonial spheres of otherness. Those who went out to confront (and to convert, to uplift, to exploit, or to destroy) 'savages' overseas did so in the context of the domestic cultural experience. . . . Both those who traveled overseas and those who read the literature they produced reacted to the experience of 'savages' abroad . . . in terms of prior experience with the changing class society of Britain" (1987:234).

Deeply implicated in the representation of cultural difference is also the representation of gender: if the novel is one constituent of empire in its particular form, the specific gender arrangements of the period are a third factor of the configuration. Although Green maintains that the "domestic" novel was a story of "sisters and their courtship" that had little to do with relationships outside the metropolis, the "domestic" was most often formulated, sustained, and tested by its definition through and in opposition to the "external," the "foreign," and the "other." The quotations from Carlyle and Conrad cited earlier provide an example of how the culture's negotiations of gender difference supplied both a model and a vocabulary for progressively constituting empire, represented here as a supine mass to be quickened by Europe's masterful manipulation of wand and pencil. Increasingly, the processes of managing empire and gender developed as a complex system of exchange and overlap, their interlocking vocabularies and discursive strategies authorizing and reinforcing each other.[11]

This connection between the two systems is laid out with startling clarity in *Three Guineas,* Woolf's critique of the role England assigned to its "daughters of educated men":

> It was with a view to marriage that her body was educated; a maid was provided for her; . . . that the fields were shut to her; that solitude was denied her—all this was enforced upon her in order that she might preserve her body intact for her husband. . . . But we are not now asking the interesting question, *what was the effect of that education upon the race? We are asking why did such an education make the person so educated consciously and unconsciously in favour of war?* . . .

Consciously she must use whatever charm or beauty she possessed
to flatter and cajole the busy men. . . . Consciously she must accept
their views, and fall in with their decrees because it was only so that
she could wheedle them into giving her the means to marry or
marriage itself. In short, all her conscious effort must be in favour
of what Lady Lovelace called "our splendid Empire." (1938:38–39;
emphasis added)

Woolf's incisive analysis here structures the gender—and class
—arrangements of the colonizing culture as an organizing and
sustaining principle of empire.[12] The relations she articulates between empire and systemic gender differentiation had been perceived even by earlier feminists like Olive Schreiner and Josephine
Butler, but they were rarely pursued in any depth.[13]

Theorizing the relations uncovered by Woolf calls for the kind
of intersecting analysis practiced most notably by Spivak. But, as
Eve Sedgwick has noted, many feminist critics "seem poised for
the moment between reading sex and reading history, at a choice
that appears (though, it must be, wrongly) to be between the
synchronic and the diachronic" (1985:13). "The subject of sex,"
Sedgwick maintains, is "an especially charged leverage point, or
point for the exchange of meanings, between gender and class
(and in many societies, race), the sets of categories by which we
ordinarily try to describe the divisions of human labor" (11). Her
analysis suggests a common marginal space occupied by "the sexual and the political" (or by the sexual and the recognized-as-
political), zones sharing contiguous and often unreliable boundaries that are subject to continual alteration.

To read the novel's management of imperial relations in the
indeterminate space off its margins is to read, concurrently, its
management of a range of political relations. Most frequently, the
inscription of empire is coded as an inscription of gender, one
occlusion enfolding the other, as in this analogy offered by Clara's
anxious father to the monstrous Sir Willoughby in Meredith's *The
Egoist* (1879):

She has perchance wrestled with her engagement, as the aboriginals
of a land newly discovered by a crew of adventurous colonists do
battle with the garments imposed on them by our considerate civilization;—ultimately to rejoice with excessive dignity in the wearing
of a battered cocked-hat and trowsers not extending to the shanks:
but she did not break her engagement, sir; and we will anticipate
that, moderating a young woman's native wildness, she may, after

the manner of my comparison, take a similar pride in her fortune in good season. (498)

Here the anxiety inherent in the project of subjugating "a young woman's native wildness," as represented in the recalcitrant Clara, within the "romance" or "heterosexual plot" that DuPlessis describes as "a trope for the sex-gender system as a whole" (1985:5) feeds readily into the discourse of pacification and the dubious perquisites conferred by "a considerate civilization."[14] The three systems—novel, gender, and empire—converge here in a complex configuration of the "political" and the "sexual," the literary and the historical, the "synchronic" and the "diachronic." It is the space of this convergence, so persistently indicated in nineteenth-century novels, that *Reaches of Empire* seeks to negotiate.

Arguably, it is an anachronism to use the term *imperialism* of any period before the last decades of the nineteenth century, since it was only after about 1870 that *imperialism* and *imperialist* began to acquire their modern meanings.[15] *Colonialism, empire,* and *imperialism,* though connected and sometimes overlapping terms, are used here to correspond to different stages in the development of empire. *Colonial* refers to the period before the consolidations of the eighteenth and early nineteenth century, when cultural and moral meanings were not yet systematically attached to the fact of conquest. The term *imperialism* is used chiefly to refer to the period after the 1870s, when competition between the various European powers led to the self-conscious articulation and aggressive promotion of a doctrine of territorial expansion and control.[16] Although *imperialism* includes colonialism, it is not exhausted by it; present-day practices of political or territorial hegemony and control are imperialist even when they do not rely on formal colonization to achieve their ends. Throughout this study, therefore, I use *empire* and *imperial* to distinguish between these two distinct stages and to refer generally to the system of beliefs attached to Victorian representations of territorial, cultural, and culturally constructed "racial" domination.

If the term *imperialism* did not yet exist in the years when the novels studied here were written, it was coming into being through the same cultural processes; formulated and contested within the same discursive milieux, the inbred, overlapping circles of Victorian opinion making. The continuing decontextualization of literature has been successful in detaching canonized texts from their everyday political concerns and characterizing the latter as trivial or irrelevant. A similar strategy has even more effectively separated imperial ideology from the sanctified realms of European high culture; a compartmentalization, Said has pointed out, that prevents us from connecting literature and empire seriously and systematically.

The same process operates even within the work of individual authors, whose writings are compartmentalized into "serious" and "not serious" categories. A classic instance of this strategy is contemporary Carlyle scholarship. A dominant intellectual influence for much of the nineteenth century, Carlyle was a staunch defender not only of empire but of the related institution of slavery. His 1848 essay "Occasional Discourses on the Negro Question" is a ferocious defense of the slave economy in the English colony of Jamaica, a document so unreasoned and unrelenting in its invective that his twentieth-century adherents have conspired to exempt it from scholarly examination.[17] But the essay, in its adoration of the strong white man as redeemer of the earth's wastelands, is different only in emphasis, not in kind, from more respectable works in Carlyle's canon, and its implications for the body of his thought cannot be simply ignored or discounted. Given the refusal of much modern scholarship to confront or even acknowledge the underlying connections between Victorian intellectual life and Victorian imperial ideology, the detail of such secret relations needs to be disclosed.

Empire, in other words, was being constituted in a complex linkage of synchronous and sometimes indistinguishable literary, intellectual, political, and military activity. If *Reaches of Empire* supplies these unrepresented or occluded aspects of the novels it examines, to "deconceal" or manifest these in criticism is not an act of restoration but of destabilization: by these insertion in an alternative register of "history," the novels, once isolated in an insular "canon," are relocated within a troubled expanse of empire. As Homi Bhabha points out, "the practical criticism of *Scrutiny* denies the cultural and historical basis of the *literary*. . . . Consequently it denies the grounds on which to pose the question of the 'colonial' in literary representation. . . . The crisis in literary and cultural values that would ensue from a reading based on questions of historical, cultural difference . . . *within* the Great Tradition generally throws such a regime of criticism and culture into disarray" (1984:102; Bhabha's emphasis).

This dis-location of the Great Tradition by posing the question of "history" is one part of the process of reading noncollusively. As Benita Parry specifies in her essay on colonial discourse, however, literature's "subtext is both a product and a projection of 'context' as well as a textual construction" (1987:48). To read that literary construct, the text's subtext, the novels are also interrogated from within. The chapters that follow are primarily "readings": case studies and discussions of individual or clusters of novels, rather than explorations of a theory of "colonial discourse." In each of these five chapters, a novel or set of novels is located in relation to one of the cruces or key tropes of empire—abolition, interracial coupling, migration and transportation, mercantile "adventuring," orientalist visions of sati and polygamy, "thuggee," and the opium trade. Each of these also intersects with the continuing organization of gender at home.

Chapter 1 discusses *Belinda,* Edgeworth's tale of fashionable London, in the context of the campaign for the abolition of the slave trade, a campaign unavoidably complicated by popular fears of bloody and vengeful risings abroad and female unrest and miscegenation at home. In chapter 2, concerns over defining "home" and the domestic are examined through the growing importance of place in several novels of Austen and Gaskell. In part, the domestic is defined through voyages, campaigns, incursions, and migrations to and from an implied but never directly represented empire. Through such delineations of space and place, I argue, empire is imaginatively annexed and "domesticated" for the English imagination, while female character is in turn established and controlled by its positioning within these newly constructed spatial economies. Chapter 3 pursues these connections between the colonial and the domestic by examining the function of mid-Victorian constructions of femininity and family within an imperial economy through readings of Dickens' *Dombey and Son* and Thackeray's *The Newcomes.* Chapter 4 considers how, in *Vanity Fair* and *Jane Eyre,* the attempt to articulate women's imprisonment within the middle-class feminine ideal popularized during the 1840s and 1850s almost inevitably implicates the counterdiscourse of feminism in an orientalist vocabulary. In chapter 5, I suggest that the incomplete *Mystery of Edwin Drood* in many ways embodies and internalizes the anxieties of engulfment, feminization, and violence cumulatively projected in the preceding chapters.

This cluster of readings does not, of course, exhaust the ways in which empire functions in the novel, nor do I suggest that the patterns I discuss occur exclusively in these texts and authors. The anxieties of engulfment, revenge, and miscegenation discernible in the subtext of *Belinda,* for instance, may be traced more plainly in Emily Brontë's Heathcliff, a dark, vengeful figure from the slave-trading city of Liverpool who invades and disinherits the remote Yorkshire households of *Wuthering Heights.* Similarly, the delicious pastoral of Eliot's *Adam Bede* is, like the achieved domestic security of *Dombey and Son,* troubled by the unassimilable story of Hetty Sorrel's "ruin" and transportation; *Pride and Prejudice* is not immune to the military and naval interests I identify as underlying *Persuasion* or Gaskell's *North and South;* Trollope's Palliser sequence and Wilkie Collins' *The Moonstone* incorporate the concerns about security and infiltration so apparent in *Edwin Drood.* More broadly, the processes that construct Australia as an unquiet grave in *Great Expectations* and *David Copperfield* underwrite and complement the establishment of home and place not only in those individual novels but in the confident *English* communities achieved, say, in Eliot's Middlemarch, Austen's Pemberley, Gaskell's Cranford, or Trollope's Barchester. Empire, in other words, is a constitutive presence, and is in turn constituted within the novel tradition as a whole, rather than in one or two selected novels.

What is offered here, then, is a strategy: *Reaches of Empire* attempts to represent a *practice* of reading "domestic" narratives within an imperial context; the choice of individual narratives indicates the range—not the limits—of that practice. In choosing to write in local and specific ways about the novels examined here, I have been guided by two considerations: first, the need to combine recent theoretical insights with historical contextualization and a responsiveness to the particularity of texts (Christian 1988, Marcus 1987); second, I am aware that in writing about nineteenth-century fiction I take on perhaps the most familiar—the most written-about as well as the most cherished—body of texts (after Shakespeare) in English literature. The detailed rereadings work to challenge familiar patterns of perceiving these novels. Although the intensive interrogation of these texts could be seen as a reinscription of their institutionalization, they are also, because of that institutionalization, especially productive sites for the posing of new questions, questions informed by a range of oppositional cultural practices from Afro-American studies, feminism, and Marxism to deconstruction.

A deceptively simple strategy for disclosing the hidden power relations of a text is suggested by Mineke Schipper, who appends a series of negative questions to a model proposed by Mieke Bal: "Who is *not* speaking? Who has *no* right to speak? Who does *not* see? Whose view is *not* expressed? Who does *not* act? Who has been deprived of the right to act? Who is powerless to act?" and "What is the speaker saying? . . . What does he consider worth including in his story? And again, what is not included?" (1985:15–16). It is with these primary questions that this study begins.

one

~

Interruption, Interpolation, "Improvement": Inscribing Abolition and "Amalgamation" in *Edgeworth's* Belinda

Here's to the next insurrection of the negroes in the West Indies.
— *SAMUEL JOHNSON*, 1777

*M*ARIA EDGEWORTH'S *Castle Rackrent* (1800) is probably the first significant English novel to speak in the voice of the colonized. The narrative voice of the illiterate Irish peasant, Thady, is, however, heavily mediated by the obviously anglicized editor who interrupts and punctuates Thady's story on every page with textual annotations, learned interpolations, and ironic "folk" anecdotes. This editorial commentary establishes, through the very "innocence" and "fidelity" of the main narrative, the inadequacy of the indigenous Irish order, preparing the way for its gradual replacement by a more efficient breed.[1] The last pages of the novel record the inevitable overthrow of the corrupt old system by the rising professional classes represented in the lawyer Jason, old Thady's heartless, educated son.

This chapter locates Edgeworth's second novel, *Belinda*, between *Castle Rackrent*, which marks the gradual anglicization of feudal Irish society, and her 1812 work *The Absentee*, which records the completion of that process. Some of the concerns of *Castle Rackrent* are carried over into *Belinda*, a novel of significant political interest easily dismissed as a conventional tale of courtship and fashionable life in the metropolis. If the narrative voices of *Castle Rackrent* counterpoise an editorial presence, established as rational, professional, and English against that of the oral, premodern, and "racially" different Thady, *Belinda,* written the following year and concerned with several revolutionary impulses of the previous decades, in some ways reverses this process through the internal tensions of its narrative. Located in the impeccable society of English country houses and London seasons, it subverts the preeminently rational, "civilized" voices of its central characters through disturbing intertextual and internal interjections of the uncontrolled, unassimilable, or politically threatening.

On her tour of the United States in the mid-1830s, Harriet Martineau registers her surprise at learning her hosts' opinion of Edgeworth, still a flourishing and much-respected author at home:

> It was in Baltimore that I heard Miss Edgeworth denounced as a woman of no intelligence, whose works could never be cared for or read again, because in Belinda, poor Juba was married, at length, to an English farmer's daughter! The incident is so subordinate that I had entirely forgotten it: but a clergyman's lady threw the volume to the opposite corner of the floor when she came to the page. As I have said elsewhere, Miss Edgeworth is worshipped throughout the United States; but it is in spite of this terrible passage,—this clause of a sentence . . . which nobody in America can tolerate, while no one elsewhere ever, I should think, dreamed of finding fault with it. (1969:231–32)

Martineau, a staunch abolitionist and "amalgamationist" as she had just been titled for her views on interracial marriage, was justly indignant, but her literary judgment was slightly off on this occasion.[2] The "clause of a sentence" had in fact been found fault with —and by the novel's weightiest critic at home. Although her first readers seem to have remained unaware of it, Edgeworth had made important changes in *Belinda* soon after the novel's appearance.[3] Sending the corrected manuscript to Anna Laetitia Barbauld for inclusion in the British Authors series the poet was editing, Edgeworth writes:

> Belinda I have taken some, and my father has taken a great deal of pains, to improve her. In the first volume, the alterations are very slight. . . . In the second volume 'Jackson' is substituted for the

husband of Lucy instead of 'Juba', many people having been scandalised at the idea of a black man marrying a white woman; my father says that gentlemen have horrors upon this subject, and would draw conclusions very unfavorable to a female writer who appeared to recommend such unions; as I do not understand the subject, I trust to his better judgment and end with—for Juba read Jackson.

(Le Breton 1874:136)

Barbauld, abolitionist and author of a poem to Wilberforce, does not appear to have commented on this improvement, perhaps because some differences of principle between the families had been long acknowledged. Mr. Barbauld, for instance, was known to provide himself with his own sugar when he went to tea with the Edgeworths so that, in Maria's words, "he might not share our wickedness in eating that made by a Negro slave" (quoted, Dykes 1942:30). Although her family counted several abolitionists among its friends, Edgeworth, fearful of gentlemenly "horrors" and less an independent woman of letters than either Barbauld or Martineau, was not ready to risk the public label of "amalgamationist." But the "better judgment" on which she was so reliant required further changes to the novel. The letter to Barbauld continues:

> In the third volume, I have taken out everything that gave encouragement (beyond esteem) to Mr Vincent, for great complaints were made against Belinda for want of constancy to Clarence Hervey, and for jilting Vincent. By taking out her consent to marry, I hope I shall in some degree, satisfy all parties. Belinda is but an uninteresting personage after all, but I cannot *mend* her in this respect without making her over again.
>
> (Quoted, Le Breton 1874:136–37)

Curtailing the possibilities of an English marriage for both black servant and Creole master, then, accomplishes the "improvement" of *Belinda,* a project occasioned chiefly by Edgeworth's anxiety about male (paternal and public) disapproval. The change also necessarily entails a curtailment of choice for the novel's heroine, since Belinda is now bound to remain irrevocably constant to her first suitor, the learned and aristocratic Englishman Clarence Hervey. Edgeworth seems to have been dissatisfied but resigned at the effect of this change on the character of her heroine. In the new and improved version of the novel, female freedom of choice is represented chiefly by the chastised rake, Lady Delacour, and the sexually and racially ambiguous "man-woman," Harriot Freke.

All editors of the novel since 1810 have retained Richard Edgeworth's corrections, and "for Juba read Jackson" has received more attention in social history than in Edgeworth criticism.[4] I suggest that what Martineau called "this . . . incident so subordinate" in fact completes otherwise obscure thematic and structural patterns in *Belinda* and relates it to the revolutionary impulses stirred by Wollstonecraftian feminism on the one hand and the revolutions in France and Haiti on the other. Most important, this censored section pulls together and makes perceptible *Belinda*'s disturbing subtext—one that, in its linking of racial and sexual anxieties, questions (but does not overthrow) the hierarchical certainties expressed by the central characters of the novel.

⤐

Published in the first year of the nineteenth century, *Belinda* is very much a novel of transition between a period of revolutionary aspiration and a century of increasingly repressive consolidation. Nowhere are the anxieties of the 1790s more evident than in the chapter that brings Belinda, the disreputable Harriot Freke, and Belinda's Creole suitor, Mr. Vincent, together to be instructed on women's happiness by the novel's Thomas Bertram figure, the enlightened patriarch and West Indian absentee landlord, Percival:

> "This is just the way you spoil women," cried Mrs Freke, "by talking to them of the *delicacy of their sex*, and such stuff. This *delicacy* enslaves the pretty delicate dears."
>
> "No; it enslaves us," said Mr Vincent.
>
> "I hate slavery! Vive la liberté!" cried Mrs Freke. "I'm a champion of the Rights of Woman."
>
> "I am an advocate for their happiness," said Mr Percival, "and for their delicacy, as I think it conduces to their happiness. . . . Fortunately for society, the same conduct in ladies which best secures their happiness most increases ours."
>
> Mrs Freke beat the devil's tattoo for some moments, and then exclaimed, "You may say what you will, but the present system of society is radically wrong:—whatever is, is wrong."
>
> (208–9)

This passage focuses several ideological anxieties that are present, though in muted form, throughout the novel. The passage—indeed, the whole chapter—has a resonance not easily explained. Colin B. Atkinson and Jo Atkinson find that "the whole scene is gratuitous not because the subject was unusual—discussions about women's rights were common—but because the sentiments expressed by Mrs Freke do not fit in with her character, nor are they prepared for in any way, nor referred to again outside the chapter" (1984:113). Confronted by the introduction of this seemingly irrelevant subject, Atkinson and Atkinson conclude: "Maria Edgeworth has contrived this debate, quite out of keeping with Mrs Freke's character, to discredit radical feminism" (109).

Percival's views in this debate are remarkably similar to those of another West Indian landowner, Sir Thomas Bertram in *Mansfield Park,* who advises Fanny Price that the "independence of spirit which prevails so much in modern days . . . in young women is offensive and disgusting beyond all common offence" (318). Margaret Kirkham's suggestive delineation of the link between abolition and feminism in *Mansfield Park* is pertinent here: "In *Mansfield Park* the English patriarch is also the owner of Antiguan plantations and of the slaves who work them. When he returns to England, his niece puts a question to him about the slave trade. We are not told what the question was, nor what answer was given, but through the title, the making of Sir Thomas a slave-owner abroad, and the unstated question of Miss Fanny, her moral status in England is implicitly contrasted yet also compared with that of Antiguan slaves" (1983:118).

Although the discussion between Freke, Belinda, and Percival is ostensibly about the "Rights of Woman" (which is also the title of the chapter), Wollstonecraft's famous 1792 text is not the only revolutionary influence at work here. Harriot Freke's language also carries disturbing reminders of abolition and insurrection into Percival's beautifully regulated domestic life.

The conjunction of the two is especially threatening because unlike the familiar, slightly eccentric, abolitionism of middle-class intellectuals like the Barbaulds, this revolutionary form is identified with the power of the slave Other itself. "Who am I? Only a Freke! shake hands" (37) is Harriot's introduction of herself, as she appears disguised in male clothes to hear a forbidden parliamentary debate.[5] In this chapter, in addition to being the "man-woman" that Vincent's black servant, Juba, identifies her as, Freke takes on a second alien identity: that of the powerful and mysterious black priestess she had earlier outlined in flames of phosphorus to terrify Juba. It is in these terms that she is dismissed by Belinda who, determinedly rational and firmly aligned with Percival on what makes for female happiness, is "not to be terrified by an obeah woman" (211).

Freke's creation of a female figure outlined in phosphorescent flames recalls other fiery manifestations of female anger and rebellion traced by Sandra Gilbert and Susan Gubar (1979); simultaneously, her choice of the obeah woman links this feminist anger to other political rebellions. Freke's defiant manifesto ("I hate slavery! Vive la liberté! I am a champion for the Rights of Woman!") invokes not only the bogey of the revolution in France and the recent anti-British rising in Ireland and its accompanying French invasion.[6] Far worse, it recalls the 1791 slave rebellion of San Domingo, which was crucially connected with the development of the French revolution (James 1963; Cooper 1988). The terrifying possibility of a Haiti-style rebellion in the English slave colonies had instantly become a national obsession, as Edgeworth's own story of slave insurrection, "The Grateful Negro," bears witness. This Moral Tale, published a year after *Belinda,* features a flesh and blood obeah woman, the ruthless "chief instigator" of a slave uprising throughout the plantations of Jamaica (1969:410). Edgeworth's unusual interest in the subject is evident in a footnote more than a page long that quotes an extract on obeah from Bryan Edwards' popular history of the West Indies. Obeah, representing as it did the survival of African religion and culture on the plantations, was immediately recognized by slave owners as a vehicle of resistance and defiance, and brutal measures were taken to crush its (often female) practitioners.[7] To the West Indian plantocracy so heavily represented in *Belinda*—Percival, Vincent, and the father of Belinda's rival, Virginia, are all owners of Caribbean properties, and Virginia's lover, Captain Sunderland, has helped suppress a slave revolt there—the obeah woman is a frightening portent indeed.

Not only are fears of slave and colonial revolt encoded within feminist ideas in this chapter, these threatening ideologies are all apprehended as part of the same upheaval. Merging such connected but distinct anxieties within the same figure makes them easier to confront but, as Atkinson and Atkinson complain, creates a character whose motivation appears contradictory.

There is some indication in Frances Edgeworth's *Memoir* of her

stepdaughter that Harriot Freke was originally conceived somewhat differently; the novel itself reveals a perceptible tension in
her characterization.[8] Like Milton's Satan, whom she quotes in her
conversation with Belinda, Freke is placed in increasingly ridiculous and humiliating situations in the last third of the text. Directly
after the argument with Percival, the insertion of a subplot involving Miss Moreton, a young lady Freke "abducts" and then encour-
ages in sexual experimentation, suggests an urgent need to under-
mine the impression Freke's revolutionary declaration might have
made.[9]

Edgeworth's treatment discredits Freke as a character while at
the same time giving her radical opinions a hearing. Such caution
can perhaps be explained by the antifeminist backlash and scandal
provoked only two years before by Godwin's candid biography of
Wollstonecraft. Although Anna Barbauld (as well as the feminist
Mary Hays) had come to Wollstonecraft's defense, Kirkham has
argued that the Great Wollstonecraft Scandal made a younger
generation of novelists—including Edgeworth, Austen, Ann Radcliffe, and Hannah More—extremely cautious about voicing feminist opinions directly (1983:49; Butler 1982:95–97).[10] Edgeworth's need to dissociate herself from Wollstonecraft and her own
ambivalence about her character's revolutionary opinions finds its
best expression perhaps in Freke's final appearance in the novel:
while lurking as an eavesdropper and voyeur (again recalling Satan) in Lady Delacour's garden, Freke is caught and lamed in a
"man-trap," a punishment that ensures she will never wear men's
clothes again.

⛯

"The year 1800–1801," Wylie Sypher writes in his study of antislavery literature, "is admittedly the darkest in abolition history"
(1969:21).[11] In 1801, the year of *Belinda's* publication, well over
half the Atlantic slave trade was still controlled by England. Wide-
spread antiabolitionism and anti-Jacobinism had followed the revolutions in France and Haiti (Sypher 1969:11–12). Wilberforce's
motion in favor of abolition had been defeated in the Commons
ten years earlier, the occasion of Anna Barbauld's "Epistle" to the
disappointed leader:

> Cease, Wilberforce, to urge thy generous aim!
> Thy country knows the sin, and stands the shame!

The Preacher, Poet, Senator in vain
Has rattled in her sight the Negro's chain.

(1825:173–79)

Somewhat like feminists in the wake of the Great Wollstonecraft Scandal, abolitionists were now widely distrusted and discredited. In the words of the activist Thomas Clarkson, "many looked upon abolitionists as monsters" (quoted, Sypher 1969:21).

This was in marked reaction to the decades of the 1770s and 1780s, when what Wordsworth called the "novel heat / Of virtuous feeling" (*The Prelude*, X:252–53) in favor of abolition had spread rapidly, for a variety of complex reasons. Tempting as it is to see the increasing enthusiasm for abolition as a tardy but laudable manifestation of humane feeling, C. L. R. James has cautioned: "Those who see in abolition the gradually awakening conscience of mankind should spend a few minutes asking themselves why man's conscience, which had slept peacefully for so many centuries, should awake just at the time that men began to see the unprofitableness of slavery as a method of production in the West Indian colonies."[12] Occasionally, abolitionist sentiments were even invoked as an argument to further colonization and the expansion of British rule (Dykes 1942:126).

But if the gathering strength of industrialization and the need for more efficient empire were part of the impetus behind abolition, some of its individual supporters were, no doubt, motivated by honorable considerations. Among the many intellectuals who had supported the cause were several figures from the Edgeworths' circle: the Barbaulds, Erasmus Darwin, Anna Seward, and —most important—Thomas Day, a minor lion of the movement since the publication of his immensely popular sentimental poem, "The Dying Negro," in 1773.[13] Day, a close friend of Edgeworth's father, is a crucial figure in her biography. It was in deference to Day's "eloquent philippic against female authorship" that Richard Edgeworth had abandoned the effort to publish his daughter's work during Day's lifetime.[14] If the secret composition of *Castle Rackrent* (the only one of her works never subjected to her father's improving hand) first enabled Edgeworth to write serious fiction, Day's death freed her to become a published author. Although Day died in 1792, his presence is as significant in *Belinda* as her father's more immediate influence.

British abolitionism was in some ways more active as a literary

than a political movement (Sypher 1969). Whether the work of
minor figures like Day and Hannah More or of the period's greatest authors, such as Cowper, Southey, and Wordsworth, however,
the huge output of literature generated by the abolitionists is
unread and almost unacknowledged in literary studies.[15] Sypher
suggests that one reason for this is the sheer badness of antislavery
writing, especially verse, and describes it as "often ethically as well
as aesthetically hollow" (1969:157), partly because of a lack of deep
engagement on the part of the writers themselves (Dabydeen
1985:43–46). Still, the most casual browsing through the work of
prominent authors between, say, the 1750s and 1807 reveals that
abolition was a persistent and significant literary concern. In addition to writing and speaking against slavery, Johnson centered
Rasselas (1759) around a black hero. Sterne preached abolitionist
sermons and included a wistful, poignant antislavery scene in *Tristram Shandy* (1759). In *Candide,* also published in 1759, Voltaire
wrote a powerful episode linking the cruelties of slavery with sugar
consumption in the salons of Europe. The hero of Mary Brunton's
recently rediscovered novel, *Discipline* (1815), is a West India pro-
prietor who speaks in parliament (like Wilberforce) against the
slave trade, then goes to work among Caribbean slaves when the
bill is defeated.[16]

The sheer number of such scenes and themes during this period suggests that abolition was something more than a chic contemporary issue "finding its way" into literature. Rather, the nu-
merous ways in which slavery and the slave trade were written
about in these years were part of the process through which the
literary forms of the day were constituting themselves, discovering
and ordering their proper concerns and boundaries, at the same
time contesting, refining, or validating existing boundaries.

It is within this literary context that the introduction of the West
Indian slave Juba and his master Vincent is important in *Belinda,*
which examines and embodies the tensions between the prevalent
anti-Jacobinism and the discredited doctrines of feminism and
abolitionism. The rich Creole and his entourage are situated within
two different schemes in the novel—one overt and explicit, the
other submerged and allusive. The first relates to the visible social
hierarchy. Percival, one of the many figures in his daughter's
works modeled on Richard Edgeworth, is not only the perfect
father, husband, and landlord, but also Vincent's mentor and
guardian. Vincent, though not as wise as Percival or his English-

born rival Clarence Hervey, is deserving enough to have the
devoted loyalty of the perfect black servant Juba, whose status
somewhere between human and animal is signified by his guard-
ianship, in turn, of the magnificent dog with whom he shares a
name:

> "I can assure your ladyship," cried Mr Vincent, "that he is the
> very quietest and best creature in the world."
> "No doubt," said Belinda, smiling, "since he belongs to you . . .
> every thing animate or inanimate that is under your protection, you
> think must be the best of its kind in the universe."
> "But, really, Juba *is* the best creature in the world," repeated Mr
> Vincent, with great eagerness. . . .
> "Juba, the dog, or Juba, the man?" said Belinda: "you know they
> cannot be both the best creatures in the universe."
> "Well! Juba, the man, is the best man—and Juba, the dog, is the
> best dog . . . " said Mr Vincent, laughing, with his usual candour, at
> his own foible, when it was pointed out to him.
>
> (315)

This conversation draws on a discourse of the humanity of slaves
and the linking of dogs and slaves in proslavery propaganda, a
relation underscored by the contemporary fashion of naming both
dogs and slaves for fallen kings (Fryer 1984:148).[17]

Just as Belinda instructs Vincent on his "foible" in relation to
the two Jubas, her example teaches him to amend his admiration
for Creole women ("all softness, grace, delicacy" and amiable in-
dolence) by observing her own superiority to them (211):

> "West-Indian ladies!" interrupted Mr Vincent. "Surely, Miss Port-
> man cannot imagine that I am at this instant thinking of any West
> Indian lady! . . . I have learnt to admire *European beauty, European
> excellence!* I have acquired new ideas of the female character."
>
> (216)

The clear superiority of *"European excellence!"* ensures, in advance
that Vincent will not prove a fit husband for Belinda. As in the
case of the dissolute antihero Staunton in Scott's *The Heart of
Midlothian* or the monstrous Bertha Mason in *Jane Eyre*, Vincent's
West Indian birth predisposes him to moral weakness.[18] Belinda's
consideration of Vincent as a suitor is allowable because, as Lady
Delacour says, "notwithstanding Mr V—is a creole, he has been
bred up by his guardian in a class of men who learn by the

experience of others" (253). In the event, Vincent's non-European birth proves stronger than Percival's influence, though the latter is explicitly exempted from all blame for his ward's moral failure. But if Vincent will never be fit to inherit the mantle of the enlightened Percival (whose true successor is Clarence Hervey), he is still a good and generous "young massa" for the two Jubas, even granting the faithful slave his freedom at the end of the first edition of *Belinda*. The hierarchy endorsed here is rendered clearly enough: white man :: Creole :: black man :: dog.

This apparently simple chain of mastery and command is, however, complicated by a second system of hidden resemblances between the various outcast figures of the novel. Harriot Freke, we have already seen, is identified with the obeah woman in her advocacy of dangerous revolutionary causes. At the same time, the text identifies her with Vincent, another non-European and consequently suspect figure, even if he is a slave-owning Creole rather than an African slave. Vincent's instinctive hostility toward Freke is noted by the omniscient Percival: "It has been remarked, that an antipathy subsists between creatures, who, without being the same, have yet a strong external resemblance" (206). This antipathy combined with resemblance between the marginal characters of the novel is again suggested in the strange encounter in Vincent's lodgings between the human Juba and the Jewish money lender Solomon:

> Terrified at the sight of the pistol, the Jew instantly explained who he was . . . but this appeared highly improbable to Juba . . . besides . . . he saw secret terror in Solomon's countenance. Solomon had an antipathy to the sight of a black, and he shrunk from the negro with strong signs of aversion. Juba would not relinquish his hold; each went on talking in his own angry gibberish as loud as he could.
>
> (404)

The visceral hostility of Solomon for Juba recalls Juba's own instinctive dislike of Freke: Vincent is amused by the simple way in which Juba "expressed his aversion of the man-woman who lived in the house with him and the odd manner in which the black imitated her voice and gesture" (200). To terrify Juba in revenge for his mimicry, Freke in turn imitates the semblance of an obeah woman, "all in flames." A circle of aversion, resemblance, and duplication works to link the figures outside the stable center of the novel—as represented by Belinda and her mentors, the Percivals—in a second, almost illicit, scheme of relationships.

The pattern of resemblance and alliance between Vincent, Juba, Solomon, and Harriot Freke (all figures who threaten by their obvious difference) can be seen as reproducing some of the ways in which the subaltern groups of nineteenth-century Britain were "metaphorically equated—if not directly, then through their mutual likeness to savages, or departure from the civilized norm, or sharing of some 'primitive' attribute" (Stocking 1987:229). These outcast groups, Stocking continues, shared not only certain mental characteristics but a social positioning.[19]

> Along different lines—of domestic life (woman, child), of socioeconomic status (laborer, peasant, pauper), of deviancy (criminal, madman), and of "race" (Celtic Irishman, black savage)—they all stood in a subordinate hierarchical relationship to those who dominated the economic life, who shared the political power, or who most actively articulated the cultural ideology of mid-Victorian Britain. Many of these relationships were not simply hierarchical, but exploitative as well, in the sense that the life possibilities of a single individual higher up were sustained by the labor of a number of people lower down the pyramid. . . . Finally these categories had in common that . . . they were kept in a status of dependency or tutelage and denied the rights of full participation in . . . modern civilization.
>
> (229–30)

The resemblance combined with revulsion that characterizes the interaction of Freke, the human Juba, Vincent, and Solomon becomes explicable by their common situation: they are linked within a scale that structures them all as outsiders yet pits them simultaneously against one another, to their collective disadvantage. Established through a network of allusions, hints, and symbolic or metaphoric equations, this connection, albeit grounded in hostility and mimicry, links the subaltern characters of *Belinda* in a system that functions as an implicit counterpart to the hierarchical social relations of empire.

⁂

Simultaneous with the novel's constituting and ordering processes is its assimilation of new cultural materials. An instance occurs in the passage where Lady Delacour, waiting impatiently for Clarence Hervey to carry out a wager by appearing in women's clothes (another of *Belinda*'s several allusions to cross-dressing), is entertained by "the purblind dowager, Lady Boucher," with the tale of a miracle drug that will prove to be the hinge of one of the subplots: "She entered into the history of the negro slave named Quassi, who discovered this medical wood, which he kept a close secret till Mr Daghlberg, a magistrate of Surinam, wormed it out of him, brought a branch of the tree to Europe and communicated it to the great Linnaeus—when Clarence Hervey was announced by the title of 'The Countess de Pomenars' " (62–63).

The dowager's history of this miracle cure, "anima of quassia," is a classic image of the cultural processing of empire: "wormed . . . out" of a slave by unspecified methods, the drug and its secret source (a tree) are brought into Europe by a colonial official and incorporated into the body of Western medical knowledge represented by "the great Linnaeus." What is not incorporated is the narrative of how the knowledge was transmitted; that story is interrupted in the telling by the central events of the novel. Its obscured history must be searched out in the gaps and interstices of the main narrative, where it seems to occur not for its own sake but to facilitate the movement of the plot.

Similarly, in displaying his conversational skills to a Spanish visitor, Hervey, "our hero, traverse[s]" the literary range: "From Twiss to Vida, from Irwin to William Jones, from Spain to India, he passed with admirable celerity, and seized all that could adorn his course from Indian Antiquities or Asiatic Researches" (99). The novel functions very much as "our hero" does here, seizing all that could adorn its course from the margins of its colonial resources. Yet might there be moments when these "seized" or "wormed out" elements of the suppressed colonial world undercut the very medium they have been appropriated into, in the same way that the non-European characters of the novel enter into disturbing patterns of alliance with all that is other and threatening within the dominant culture itself?

To pursue this line of questioning, I return now to the occluded, "subordinate incident," suppressed (though not invisible) in all but the first edition of *Belinda,* with which this chapter began: the marriage of the (barely?) human Juba to Lucy, the English farmer's daughter. Belinda's introduction to Lucy's history occurs in a significant context. The perfect Lady Anne Percival, who has succeeded Lady Delacour as Belinda's patroness (as she succeeded her in Percival's affections) is trying to convince Belinda that second thoughts in love are usually better. This is not a surprising position for Lady Anne, considering that she herself is Percival's second choice, but Belinda, the model of feminine prudence, remains unconvinced. The morning after their conversation the two women meet Lucy, whose story must be read while mentally reversing Edgeworth's 1810 instruction, "for Juba read Jackson":

> "Well, Lucy," said Lady Anne, "have you overcome your dislike to James Jackson?"
>
> The girl reddened, smiled, and looked at her grandmother, who answered for her in an arch tone, "Oh, yes, my lady! We are not afraid of Jackson *now;* we are grown very great friends. . . . Indeed he's a most industrious, ingenious good-natured youth; and our Lucy takes no offence at his courting her now, my lady, I can assure you. . . . So I tell him he need not be discouraged . . . for she's a good girl and a sensible girl . . . and the eyes are used to a face after a time, and then its nothing."
>
> (222–23)

The abrupt introduction of "James Jackson" and the several unexplained references in the passage ("we are not afraid of Jackson *now,*" "the eyes are used to a face after a time") suggest that Juba's presence is only incompletely obliterated.[20]

In the following chapter, the wedding of Lucy and "Jackson" is presented as an idyllic scene of English pastoral:

> One fine morning, Lady Anne Percival came into Belinda's room with a bridal favour in her hand. "Do you know," said she, "that we are to have a wedding today? . . . Lucy . . . is the bride, and James Jackson is the bride-groom. Mr Vincent has let them a pretty little farm in the neighbourhood. . . . "
>
> They looked out of the window and saw a troop of villagers, gaily dressed, going to the wedding . . . and all the rural company were invited to a dance in the evening . . . Belinda heard from all sides praises of Mr Vincent's generosity . . . Juba had composed, in his broken dialect, a little song in honour of his master, which he sang to his banjore with the most touching expression of joyful gratitude.
>
> (235)

The 1810 insertion is plainly visible, and again the substitution of Jackson for Juba seems half-hearted and incomplete. The black servant with his "banjore" remains the hero of the English country wedding, and his Creole master its patron, even when the former's role as bridegroom is superficially written out.

With some gentle hints from Lady Anne, Belinda applies the lesson of Lucy's change of heart to her own case and begins to reconsider the possibility of substituting Vincent for Hervey (for Hervey read Vincent?). This possibility she had rejected decidedly earlier in the novel, responding in highly significant terms to Lady Anne's suggestion that she might become accustomed to her new suitor: " 'Accustomed!' said Belinda, smiling, '. . . but at this rate, my dear Lady Anne, I do not doubt but one might grow accustomed to Caliban' " (221).

Edgeworth's breathlessly apologetic explanation for Belinda's acceptance of Vincent after this suggests that her critics had found her change of heart particularly objectionable:

> We have detailed Lady D's recovery, and we have added a few sentences to explain that Belinda would have loved Clarence better than any other person *always* if he had declared any attachment to her, but that she had turned her thoughts *from* him when he made no declaration of love to her—In the last scene he is *now* made distinctly to avow his passion for her—There are many other faults but we did not think it would be wise to botch."
>
> (quoted, Butler, 1972:494)

Does the intense discomfort both Edgeworth and her critics seem to have felt over Belinda's change of heart indicate that it was construed as a kind of "grow[ing] accustomed to Caliban?" I have already suggested that Vincent, despite his wealth and charm, is linked to the suspect manifestations of the Other in the novel. The critical clamor for Belinda's perfect fidelity might, in this case, have concealed resistance to the idea of the Creole Vincent as (even temporarily) an accepted lover; a resistance stemming from the same source as the objections to Juba as Lucy's bridegroom. There is no doubt that such objections could be extremely virulent, as in this passage by the emergent "radical," William Cobbett:

> Who, that has any sense or decency, can help being shocked at the familiar intercourse, which has gradually been gaining ground, and which has, at last, got a complete footing between the Negroes and the women of England? No black swain need, in this loving country, hang himself in despair . . . if he be not a downright cripple, he will, if he be so disposed, always find a woman, not merely to yield to his

filthy embraces . . . but to accompany him to the altar, to become his wife, to breed English mulattoes, to stamp the mark of Cain upon her family and her country! Amongst white women, this disregard of decency, this defiance of the dictates of nature, this foul, this beastly propensity, is, I say it with sorrow and with shame, *peculiar to the English.*

(1804:935)

Written three years after the publication of *Belinda,* Cobbett's piece displays all the masculine "horrors" Richard Edgeworth had foreseen. "By the 1790s," Peter Fryer has shown, the prospect of abolition had made "the 'taint' of intermarriage . . . an obsession with the propagandists of racism" (1984:163–64). Catherine Gallagher has described Cobbett as one of several social critics who "appropriated the images, the rhetoric, and the tone of the anti-slavery movement" (1985:4–9) to express a mounting opposition to industrialism but who were simultaneously themselves support-ers of slavery. Drawing on the rhetoric of retribution and revenge adopted by abolitionism itself, antiabolitionists like Cobbett iden-tify the bodies of its women as the means through which England's territory is now threatened and invaded, as vengeful slaves "amal-gamate" with Englishwomen to "stamp the mark of Cain upon her family and her country."

But if two controversial pairings between English women and non-Europeans were occluded in later editions of *Belinda* because of the spoken and unspoken anxieties accompanying abolition, a third seems to have escaped hostile detection. This thwarted mar-riage emerges in the discussion of Day's poem "The Dying Negro" in the last chapters of the novel. The topic is very cleverly intro-duced as a literary one, through which Lady Delacour attempts to measure Vincent's critical judgment against that of the brilliant Hervey, the suitor she prefers for Belinda:

> To make her peace with Mr Vincent . . . her ladyship now turned the conversation from Juba the dog, to Juba the man. She talked of Harriot Freke's phosphoric Obeah woman. . . . From thence she went on to the African slave trade, by way of contrast, and she finished precisely where she intended and where Mr Vincent could have wished, by praising a poem called 'The dying Negro' which he had the previous evening brought to read to Belinda.

(317)

Day's poem was based on a real-life incident reported in a contemporary newspaper: "A Black, who a few days before ran away from his master, and got himself christened, with intent to marry his fellow-servant, a white woman; being taken, and sent on board the Captain's ship in the Thames took an opportunity of shooting himself in the head."[21] The incident provoked outrage because it took place in 1773, one year after the celebrated Mansfield Judgment had supposedly abolished slavery on English soil.[22] The poem's extended title was "The Dying Negro, a Poetical Epistle Supposed to be written by a Black . . . to his intended wife."

Vincent's choice of this poem as a gift for Belinda is clearly not accidental. The tragic end of the projected "amalgamationist" marriage in "The Dying Negro," is one of a series of thwarted pairings between European and colonial alien canvassed throughout the novel. In the case of Vincent and Belinda, the imperial hierarchy the novel has established ensures in advance the impossibility of their marriage. Yet, the novel's marginal references—first in the obscured story of Juba and Lucy, then in the instance of "The Dying Negro"—continue to hint at its possibility, if not its fulfillment. In this buried reference can be perceived the tension between the imperatives of political orthodoxy and the transgressive and revolutionary aspirations the novel is simultaneously interrogating.

The occasion for the poem's introduction is equally significant. Vincent's offering is meant to demonstrate the quality of his literary judgment as compared to that of his learned rival. Hervey, we have seen, is a skilled orientalist, adorning his sparkling discourses with what he can mine "from Indian Antiquities or Asiatic Researches" (99); Vincent's choice, on the other hand, simply "breathes . . . the manly, energetic spirit of virtue" (318) of Day's poem. The introduction of his poem now allows Day to make a direct appearance in the text. Whereas the brilliant Hervey has been imitating one of Day's less successful projects in an absurd scheme to educate his prospective wife, Virginia, in strict isolation, the racially and morally suspect Vincent introduces Day at his best, as the poet of "The Dying Negro."

Hervey's experiment of educating Virginia in seclusion is based on an unfortunate real-life attempt by Day to educate a wife for himself on Rousseau's principles (Butler 1972:39, 243). At the end of *Belinda,* Hervey is reinstated and absolved of guilt in the Virginia episode only after affirming Day's solemn imprecation against seducers of women. This absolution then extends, by implication, to the poet himself, since Hervey's initial offense was itself an imitation of Day's. Day had dedicated the first edition of "The

Dying Negro" to Rousseau, "whose virtue is as unequalled as his genius, and whose life is a nobler pattern of imitation than his writings." In *Belinda,* Day's writings become a nobler pattern of imitation than his paternalistic and misogynistic life, allowing Edgeworth's text to simultaneously acknowledge and rebuke her early mentor.[23]

$\mathcal{J}\!\!\!\!\!\frown$

"What begs to be explained in a work," Pierre Macherey has said,

> is not that false simplicity which derives from the apparent unity of its meaning, but the presence of a relation, or an opposition, between elements of the exposition or levels of composition, those disparities which point to a conflict of meaning. This conflict is not the sign of an imperfection; it reveals the inscription of an *otherness* in the work, through which it maintains a relationship with that which it is not, that which happens to be at its margins. . . . The book is furrowed by the allusive presence of those other books against which it is elaborated. . . . The book is not the extension of a meaning, it is generated from the incompatibility of several meanings.
>
> (1978;79–80)

I have tried to link *Belinda*'s persistent interest in the disturbing topics of slave rebellion and abolition, "amalgamation," and feminist aspiration, into a coherent subtext that undercuts, or at least unsettles, the novel's putative assumptions and indicates its obscured relation with "that which it is not." The novel connects challenges to hierarchical and colonizing systems by alluding repeatedly to the possibility of alliances, sexual and other, between the repressed classes (women, menials, blacks, and other non-Europeans) of nineteenth-century England—connections that are revealed in its layers of intertextual allusion, "improvement," and accretion, and the incomplete overwriting of its original plot. The texts it engages directly and indirectly range from Wollstonecraft's *Vindication of the Rights of Woman* to Rousseau's *Emile* (and its tropical offshoot, Saint-Pierre's *Paul et Virginie*) as well as the range of proslavery and antislavery writing from Bryan Edwards' *History* to Day's *The Dying Negro.*

Also necessarily a part of this intertextual field are Edgeworth's own fictions of Ireland and the West Indies. *Castle Rackrent,* the first important novel to employ the narrative voice of the colonized, engages with its colonial setting in a way that provided a model not only for Scott's more influential "national" novels but for representing colonial relations elsewhere in the empire. Stocking points out that "Ireland since Elizabethan times provided a mediating exemplar for both attitudes and policy in relations with 'savages' overseas" (1987:234); Edgeworth's 1812 tale, *The Absentee,* explicitly refers to the similarities between the Irish and West Indian situations (1969b:129).[24] Between these two Irish novels is another of Edgeworth's stories set in an English colony, "The Grateful Negro," a Moral Tale of slave rebellion in Jamaica. "The Grateful Negro" was published a year after *Belinda,* and the novel of imperial metropolis and the tale of a slave colony have, as we have already seen, at least one character, the fiery Obeah Woman, in common. "The Grateful Negro" ends with full-scale revolution narrowly averted by the efforts of its hero, a noble slave named Caesar. But Caesar's efforts come too late to stop the rebellion completely: some of the slaves rise "in a body; and before they could be prevented . . . they had set fire to the overseer's house and the canes. The overseer . . . died in tortures, inflicted by the hand of those who had suffered most by his cruelties" (1969a:418–19).

Sypher and Howard Temperley have both discussed the decline of antislavery writing in the aftermath of the Haitian Revolution; according to Temperley, even staunch abolitionists were now reluctant to express support for open rebellion (1972:76–77). Indeed, Sypher reports that after 1791 abolition ceased to be a popular literary theme, whereas defenders of slavery become much more active in literature (1969:10). Edgeworth's Moral Tale, though overtly cautionary, advocating kindness and generosity as the best means of avoiding rebellion, disputes this trend by suggesting a certain understanding for the rebels; the contemporary horror and moral condemnation at the very idea of a slave uprising is less evident here.

In *Belinda,* the notion of revolution is a more disturbing and threatening one, yet the novel acknowledges it, however obliquely and disquietingly. In his book on Edgeworth's politics, Michael Hurst has compared her view of the colonial relationship with that of her contemporary James Mill on India: "In the ultimate analysis . . . she was always aiming to remain a 'Friend of the People' and its untiring guide rather than the instrument of profound social revolution leading on to a transference of political authority into 'native' hands. She made the very best of being an 'intelligent insider' and dreamed of what today would be called racial integration with all the essential features of the old order unchanged" (1969:23–24). Edgeworth's writings certainly do not suggest that she chose to become an agent of "profound social revolution"; in later years, she even took pains to dissociate herself from the radical connections made earlier in her career, regretting, for example, that her first novels were brought out by Joseph Johnson, publisher also of the "seditious and sectarian" works of Wollstonecraft, Godwin, and Blake.[25] Yet this ought not negate the impulses of liberation that do inform her work, suggesting its complicated relation with "that which it is not." *Belinda* reveals deep anxiety about the possibility of revolution but also allows for the expression and interrogation of the insurrectionary aspirations embodied in feminism, abolition, and "amalgamation."

When *Popular Tales* was published in 1804, Edgeworth's first serious reviewer, Francis Jeffrey, had been worried enough to declare acidly in the *Edinburgh Review:* "an attempt, we think, superior in genius as well as utility to the laudable exertions of Mr Thomas Paine to bring disaffection and infidelity within the comprehension of the common people, or the charitable endeavours of Messrs. Wirdsworth [*sic*] and Co. to accommodate them with an appropriate vein of poetry" (quoted, Butler 1972:339–40). This might not be enough to suggest that Edgeworth would have joined Johnson in his toast to slave insurrection had she been permitted by age and gender to be among the scholarly company at Oxford in 1777.[26] But we may acknowledge that in the tensions and contradictions of her early novel at least, the possibilities of revolutionary challenge to empire are canvassed and—precariously, intermittently—acknowledged.

two

Proper Places: Spatial Economies in Austen and Gaskell

> *In this way, a network of names defined a geograph-
> ical region strategically, historically, as a place whose
> relations made travel possible and settling imminent.
> . . . [It] brought into being a country that readers
> could imagine, and therefore inhabit.*
> —PAUL CARTER,
> THE ROAD TO BOTANY BAY

*T*HE DIVERSE fictional genres of the early nineteenth century
are preeminently interested in *place*, with grounding their various
"tales" and "romances" in specifically constituted geographical regions that then become the locus of particular moral and cultural
values. This concern with location operates in a range of ways:
negatively, by demarcating the "non-British" or "un-English"; by
incorporation, affirming the "Britishness" of marginal or unas-
similated cultures, like those of Ireland or Scotland; and by the
invention or reification of a green and rural core, which serves as
a touchstone of the truly "English."[1] The overlap and confusion of
names here itself indicates the problematic nature of national identity
in the early years of the century. In 1800 the "Act of Union"
between Ireland and Great Britain (England, Scotland, Wales) had
brought into being the official amalgam known as "The United
Kingdom." Simultaneously, rivalry with France and military expansion in India, the Caribbean, and elsewhere reinforced the
need for a common, non-European, national consciousness, while
settlements in North America, Australia, and the West Indies had

already made familiar the concept of a "Greater Britain" acquired through colonization.[2]

These complex nationalizing impulses are all represented in the various forms of the emergent novel. In the first decades of the nineteenth century, the boundaries of the newly united kingdom, Ireland and Scotland, were explored in several regional or "national" novels. The first of these, Edgeworth's *Castle Rackrent,* skillfully enacts the process of anglicization: the translation of the illiterate Thady's tale into a written and annotated narrative complements the transfer of power from a decadent Irish gentry to the anglicizing professional bourgeoisie. Inspired by Edgeworth's example, Scott wrote to praise her for "raising your national character and making the rest of the British Empire acquainted with the peculiar and interesting character of a people too long neglected and too severely oppressed" (quoted, Clarke 1949:58); a few years later, contemporary reviewers were crediting Scott's representations of cultural confrontation and reconciliation between modern England and romantic, premodern Scotland with completing the Union between those two states.

Whereas fictions of reconciliation and incorporation (Scott's *Waverley,* Edgeworth's *The Absentee*) have been, hardly coincidentally, the survivors of the "National" school, works such as Sydney Owenson's *The Wild Irish Girl: A National Tale* (1806) and Jane Porter's *The Scottish Chiefs* (1810) express a more assertive national consciousness. Owenson's insistence that contemporary Irish life "in all its combinations, can only be an example of political error" (quoted, Spender 1986:311) informs her defiant epistolary novel, addressed by the young narrator to an English M.P. Owenson focuses on the historical and cultural facts of colonization more determinedly than either Edgeworth or Scott, comparing English actions in Ireland with the notorious details of Spanish conquest in South America. Yet even Owenson's fiercely anti-English *National Tale* ends in a fantastic acceptance of metropolitan rule as the disinherited Irish princess of the title marries an English earl's heir.

Like the "National" or historical tale, English Romanticism was interested in nationalist assertions both on the European mainland (France, Greece, Germany) and in the colonized territories of Haiti and Ireland, though difference and transgression, rather than reconciliation or incorporation, were its main focus.[3] By contrast, the Gothic novel, forerunner of Romanticism, was concerned with the less complex task of delineating a generic non-British sensibility. Most of Ann Radcliffe's novels have Catholic or medieval settings, characterized by "un-English" intrigue and sensationalism, as does the best-known work of the West Indian absentee landowner, Matthew "Monk" Lewis; Charles Maturin's later Gothic classic, *Melmoth the Wanderer* (1820), is set in Ireland, Spain, and an unnamed Indian island. If the Gothic romance, impelled by the interest in national identity, explored the cultural and moral boundaries of the non-British world, its companion genre was the "Oriental Tale." Informed by a growing discourse of scholarly orientalism, this widely practiced genre was central to the delineation of the "non-European." Originally a French and German form, the Oriental Tale was employed in England by several major writers, both to define the domestic ideal (by moralists like Johnson, Addison, and Goldsmith) and in works of Romanticism and Exoticism such as Southey's *The Curse of Kehama* (1810), Moore's *Lallah Rookh* (1817), and Byron's *The Giaour* and *The Corsair* (1813). What these diverse works have in common is their imagined "oriental" setting immediately signifying radical difference and, as a necessary consequence, indubitable moral inferiority (Bearce 1961:105–10).[4]

If location and national identity were formative forces in the various subgenres of the nineteenth-century novel, a major source of this nationalizing imperative was a sense of moral distinctiveness as the colonialism of previous decades developed into a full-blown doctrine of empire based on the cultural—rather than the military—superiority of Britain. In the aftermath of the Hastings trial, for example, maintaining the profitability of the Company's interests in India became increasingly identified with the promotion and defense of British values and institutions at home as well as abroad (Bearce 1961:39–40). The definition of national character, institutionalized through the Company's creation at Haileybury of its own academy for an imperial ruling class, became inextricably linked with the accumulation and consolidation of the places and territories of empire.[5]

The development of this relationship is evident in the growing confidence with which foreign territories were incorporated into the larger narrative of British history. In his seventeenth-century travel anthology, *Purchas his Pilgrimage,* Samuel Purchas had tried to reconcile varying European accounts of the place "India":

As is observed out of *Eusebius,* the Ethiopeans arose from the river Indus. . . . Perhaps they brought the Indian name also to these parts. Or else the ignorance of those remote countries might doe it: in which respect, not only a third part of the olde world, but another new-found world, is named India. Therefore *Acosta* esteemeth India to be a generall name to all countries which are far off, and strange to vs, although it be properly attributed to the East Indies.

(1613:559)

Writing in 1613, Purchas is uneasily aware of at least two Indias, both produced out of the same European texts. The first is "properly attributed" to a specific location; the second, "a generall name to all countries which are far off, and strange to vs." Though fortified by Eusebius and Acosta, authorities of a shared tradition, it is with a certain tentativeness that Purchas names "India" from and for the known ground of Europe.

Two centuries later, James Mill, self-styled "progenitor" of the British authorized version of Indian history, was much more confident of the function of "India" in the grand narrative of Europe.[6] His 1815 essay, "On Education," cites as a blueprint for general education in England a plan originally developed by Baptist missionaries in India. The scheme, expounded in a long footnote, began with an "abstract of the solar system . . . followed by a compendious view of geography" in which "it would be *proper* to describe Europe particularly, because of its importance in the present state of the world; and Britain might, *with propriety,* be allowed to occupy . . . that pre-eminence among the nations which the God of Providence has given her" (1969:109; emphasis added). A "compendium of history and chronology united" was to be added to this providential and proper cosmography; beginning with the biblical episodes of the creation, the fall, and the flood, "the compiler" was to continue by melding secular and scriptural chronologies:

[He] should particularly notice the nations of the East, *incorporating in their proper place,* the best accounts we now have of India and China. He should go on to notice the call of Abraham . . . the Trojan war, the advent of the Saviour of men, the invention of printing, of gunpowder, and the mariner's compass, the Reformation, the discovery of the passage to India by sea, and the . . . discoveries of modern science.

(110; emphasis added)

This battery of providential dispensations, each described "in a concise but perspicuous sentence," would, the proposal concludes, "exceedingly enlarge [the student's] ideas relative to the world, certainly not to the disadvantage of Britain" (110). If Purchas, conscious of a disjunction between the naming of "India" relative to Europe and the place to which the name might be "properly attributed," conceded uncertainty about the originary stories of countries "far off, and strange to vs," two centuries later, Mill's schema comfortably incorporates those countries "in their proper place" in Britain's own story of secular and spiritual progress. In this sense, Mill's project amounts to no less than a cultural remapping of the cosmos, with geographical, historical, and theological "compendiums" of knowledge converging to establish England in its proper place of absolute centrality.

Simultaneously, the exceeding enlargement of "ideas relative to the world, certainly not to the disadvantage of Britain" was occurring within very different stories; the story, for example, of the provincial and unworldly Musgroves in Austen's *Persuasion*. The various moves and internal migrations of the novel bring the Musgroves, carefully placed in the text as prosperous farmers just emerging into gentility, within the orbit of the naval Crofts and Wentworths, the new and rising caste of empire. Mrs. Croft's expanded world directly confronts that of the static Mrs. Musgrove when the two women attempt to converse:

> "What a great traveler you must have been, ma'am!" said Mrs Musgrove to Mrs Croft.
> "Pretty well, ma'am, in the fifteen years of my marriage. . . . I have crossed the Atlantic four times and have been once to the East Indies and back again. . . . But I never went beyond the Streights— and never was in the West Indies. We do not call Bermuda or Bahama, you know, the West Indies."
> Mrs Musgrove had not a word to say in dissent; she could not accuse herself of having ever called them anything in the whole course of her life.
>
> (1984:94)

The text seizes on the contrast between the relative mobility of Mrs. Croft, one of Austen's rare happily married women, and the speechless Mrs. Musgrove, whose unaesthetic and inarticulate sighs have already provoked the narrator to a half-penitent "ridicule" (92). But more important is the act of locating performed here.

Mrs. Croft's confident assertion that "We" do not call Bermuda or Bahama "the West Indies" is part of a much wider assertion of discursive power: the proper naming of places in relation to an implicit but indisputable English center.

Similarly (though more elaborately) Scott's *The Heart of Midlothian* (1818) confirms and establishes the power relations between metropolis and hinterland by describing Jeanie Deans' journey from a prison cell in Scotland to the royal court of London. To plead at Hampton Court for the reprieve of a dissenting Scottish shepherd's daughter, Jeanie traverses not only a spatial but a cultural distance, a distance that establishes the true heart of her story *outside* the setting announced in its title. Although Jeanie's arduous passage from Midlothian to London and back reverses the direction of several other voyages in the nineteenth-century novel, it reinforces the same organization of space and power. Both Scott's novel and the extract from Austen reveal the ways in which the places of empire are named, constituted, and located in a specific relation to the metropolis; their function is to demarcate, from outside, the narrative's proper center. What happens outside or on the edges of these limits appears to occur within another frame of reference—for example, of "magic," "difference" (in the case of Scott), or invisibility—from the rest of the text. Within this reordered world, textual and geographical margins often (though not always) coincide; England is the center of the text, as of the cosmos, with the outer limits, necessary and present, incorporated in their proper places.[7]

In the rest of this chapter, I consider the organization of such marginal places in the economy of particular nineteenth-century novels and connect them to the related discourses of national identity, cultural mission, and imperial expansion. Placed within this frame, the changing interests and the neglected formal and structural characteristics of nineteenth-century fiction acquire new significance, as do hitherto inexplicable or invisible elements. The emergent castes of empire, usually identified as irrelevant and ephemeral "types"—comic nabobs or acerbic generals—turn out to include characters of far greater impact in midcentury novels— sailors, industrialists, merchants—whose assimilation is often accomplished through feminine influence, by marriage and moral education. Nancy Armstrong has suggested that the main achievement of the novel was to control and subordinate other political relations by recasting them as individual sexual relations based on a carefully constructed ideal of middle-class femininity (1987:4). If female protagonists, either as sensitive moral judges (like Anne Elliot in *Persuasion* and Margaret Hale in *North and South*) or as misguided unfortunates (like Mary Barton in Gaskell's 1848 novel) are the chief producers of cultural meaning in these texts, their positioning within certain imperial economies, I suggest, increasingly defines that meaning.

✖

"It is possible," Nina Auerbach has compellingly established, "to perceive Jane Austen's canon as one long, and always doomed, fight for escape" (1981:23)—her formulation, within the constraints of gender and class, of the condition of Romantic Imprisonment more flamboyantly represented by her male contemporaries. In the same collection of essays, Ann Banfield demonstrates equally brilliantly Austen's reshaping of the Gothic novel of place: " 'Place' became not far-away and long-ago, not continental, medieval, Catholic and feudal, but domesticated, English, modern and, ultimately, bourgeois . . . the land structured by the shaping hand or eye, nature made at once aesthetic and social, nature, 'influenced', 'improved', conquered and nationalised" (1981:31). If, as Auerbach and Banfield suggest, Austen's novels invoke both imprisonment and affirmation, comfort and confinement, the balance of this achievement depends largely on the careful delineations of place and the range of implication and association in terms like *national, English, home;* a vocabulary informed both by a discourse of expansion and by the process of Britain's moral well as geographical consolidation as an imperial power.

This process is apparent even in the typically "domestic" and pastoral scenes of a landlocked narrative like *Emma,* the only Austen novel in which the heroine undertakes no significant journeys. The panorama confronting Emma as she walks the grounds of Donwell (that medieval abbey improved into a thriving country estate) seems to exude cultural reassurance: "a sweet view, sweet to the eye and the mind. English verdure, English culture, English comfort, seen under a sun bright, without being oppressive" (1985:352). But if, as the narrative insists, the landscape is not oppressive, the situation certainly is so. Emma, briefly released from the querulous Mr. Woodhouse, explores Donwell much as Elizabeth does Pemberley in *Pride and Prejudice,* her feeling for its master being imperceptibly altered by the values embedded in his property: "It was just what it ought to be, and it looked what it was —and Emma felt an increasing respect for it, as the residence of a family of true gentility" (353). As Donwell compels her respect by its correspondence to the archetypal country house ("It was just what it ought to be, and it looked what it was"), Emma is forced to reevaluate her sister's choice of husband: John Knightley, like his magisterial brother, has "some faults of temper" but represents an alliance with "neither men, nor names, nor places, that could raise a blush" (353). Again, the testimony is negative and circular. The impression of constraint grows as Emma's brief respite of walking freely around the grounds with her "pleasant feelings" gives way to the sense that "it was necessary to do as the others did, and collect around the strawberry beds" (353). If the scene marks a change in Emma's attitude to Knightley (her "pleasant feelings"), the movement of the passage suggests at the same time that there are few other directions open to her. The almost palpable affirmations emanating from Donwell become constraining as well as reassuring, like the multiple reiterations of "sweetness" and "Englishness" in the landscape.

Emma is not the only Austen heroine to experience the English environment as circumscribing, oppressive, or threatening. It is interesting, for example, to counterpoint this scene in *Emma* with Kirkham's play on the yearning for fresh air among the confined women of *Mansfield Park* (Kirkham 1983:118–19). In 1772, the Mansfield Judgment, a landmark antislavery decision, had revived an Elizabethan decree that English air was too pure for slaves to breathe in. In the English air of Mansfield Park, however, Fanny, dependent for health and exercise on Edmund's generosity, wilts and declines when he restricts her use of his pony; as she does so once more when she is enclosed in her parents' small house in the seaside city of Portsmouth. Again, at the grand country estate of Sotherton, Maria Bertram, struggling to escape from her stifling engagement, finds—unlike Emma—no reassurance in the sweet English prospect: "Yes, certainly the sun shines and the park looks very cheerful. . . . But unluckily that iron gate . . . give[s] me a feeling of restraint and hardship. I cannot get out, as the starling said" (127).

If both *Emma* and *Mansfield Park* subtly evoke the confinement of English village life, where houses are obsessively secured and country walks circumscribed by real and imagined dangers—while Emma herself has never seen the sea—*Persuasion* appears at first as a novel of frequent and widening movement, galvanized by the influx of wealth and energy following naval victories in Europe, the Caribbean, and India. An incidental question of Mrs. Price's in *Mansfield Park*—"How could a boy be sent out to the East?" (43)—becomes a major theme in Austen's last completed novel. Although William Price's career feeds into the discussion of vocation in *Mansfield Park,* apart from Lady Bertram's stipulation that her nephew bring her *two* shawls if he should go to the East Indies, the question of what William does as a sailor receives little attention in the earlier text (except for the brief envy his adventures arouse in the idle Henry Crawford). *Persuasion,* by contrast, revels in the details of a naval career: navy lists, particulars of ships and promotions, and postings to the West Indies, Gibraltar, and other parts of the empire are eagerly discussed by the sympathetic characters, and a scorecard is kept of Wentworth's "successive captures" and prize monies, "besides the chance of what might be done in any future war" (99).[8]

This growing visibility of the navy in *Mansfield Park* and *Persuasion* supplements the increasing presence of empire at the edges of Austen's texts; progressively, her "3 or 4 Families in a Country Village," (1952:401) come to encompass and incorporate more extensive portions of the globe. The spatial interrelation between country village and colonies is enacted in the texts through the working out of new sets of social relationships. Although the most central of these is marriage, in *Mansfield Park, Persuasion,* and *Sanditon* these new relationships encompass the range of moral and material transactions involved in Austen's "continual making and remaking" (Williams 1973:113) of families, houses, estates and, finally, places.

In *Persuasion,* the conflict between new and old is one of continuity and inheritance. At the beginning of the novel, Sir Walter Elliot's extravagance forces him to lease his ancestral estate of Kellynch Hall to Admiral Croft. The transfer symbolizes a significant shift. If Sir Walter is "a foolish spendthrift baronet, who had not had principle or sense enough to maintain himself in the situation in which Providence had placed him" (250), the Admiral's conquests at sea establish his better title to the stewardship of Kellynch, "the greatest prize of all, let him have taken ever so many before" (47). Like the prize monies won for captured ships, Kellynch Hall is the rightful bounty of success at sea. The accommodation of the old land-based gentry—represented by Sir Walter and by Lady Russell—to Croft and his brother officers is completed in the courtship plot of the novel: Wentworth, "with five-and-twenty thousand pounds, and as high in his profession as merit and activity could place him" (250), is accepted at last as a fit suitor for Anne, while her patience and moral awareness in turn moderate and correct his sailor-like rashness. Anne's marriage to the self-made Wentworth rather than to her father's elegant heir represents the refurbishing of material and moral values as the old provincial breed is improved by this professional and national-minded stock.[9]

Such changes wrought in country places by seemingly distant developments in the empire are central to *Mansfield Park, Persuasion,* and *Sanditon.* Said and others have discussed the significance of Sir Thomas' unspecified but crucial Antiguan holdings to the continuity of Mansfield Park.[10] *Sanditon,* the densely organized fragment Austen was writing at the time of her death, indicates an even more direct attempt to engage with and assess the impact of these unseen forms of wealth on the internal organization of country places. In the early chapters, Lady Denham, the bustling and arrogant Catherine de Bourgh figure of *Sanditon,* complains that the new prosperity created by empire threatens old social distinctions and is barely reassured by the cheery trickle-up philosophy of the eager Mr. Parker:

> "Because they have full purses [they] fancy themselves equal, maybe, to your old county families. But . . . they never think of whether they may not be doing mischief of raising the price of things—and I have heard that's very much the case with your West-injines. . . ."
>
> "My dear madam, they can only raise the price of consumable articles, by such an extraordinary demand for them, and such a diffusion of money among us, as must do us more good than harm. —Our butchers and bakers . . . cannot get rich without bringing prosperity to *us.* If they do not gain, our rents must be insecure— and in proportion to their profit must be ours eventually in the increased value of our houses."
>
> (180)

Although *Sanditon* is unfinished, the existing chapters indicate that the conflict between new and old families would once more be worked out through the relations of courtship and marriage. The fragment introduces Austen's only major non-English character, a "half-mulatto" heiress, Miss Lambe, whose "chilly and tender" constitution may be taken as an indication of her character (205). Like Rhoda Swartz, the "West India heiress" of *Vanity Fair* who owns "a deal of money in the funds; and three stars to her name, in the East India stockholders' list" (244), Miss Lambe seems destined to be pursued and taken as a legitimate prize by the impoverished gentry of England.

Although *Persuasion* preserves a careful silence on the possible corrupting effects of the new imperial wealth (except in the ambiguous Mrs. Smith episode), and *Sanditon* can only begin to hint at its effects, the characteristically inflammatory rhetoric in a passage by Cobbett suggests the ambivalence produced in some quarters by the recent infusion of money. Cobbett describes his excursion to the new resort town of Cheltenham, "which is what they call a *'watering place'*; that is to say, a place, to which East India plunderers, West India floggers, English tax-gorgers, together with gluttons, drunkards, and debauchees of all descriptions . . . resort, at the suggestion of silently laughing quacks. . . . To places like this come . . . young wife-hunters . . . and young husband hunters . . . the former resolutely bent, be the means what they may, to give . . . heirs to their lands and tenements" (402). Austen's fragment indicates that Sanditon represents a similar gathering of the parasitic and corrupt, a kind of boomtown fed by the profits of imperial success, while Cobbett's characterization of the "heirs to the . . . lands and tenements," of the old gentry comments on the social transactions of *Mansfield Park* and *Persuasion,* as the more respectable of the new contenders, the younger Prices (Fanny, William, and Susan) and the Croft and Wentworth descendants, come into their own.

If the new relations of empire sometimes enlarge the world of Austen's novels, *Sanditon* suggests that these changes do not always promise unbounded profit or improvement. Judith Weissman, among others, has suggested that in *Persuasion* Austen discards the "counterrevolutionary" ideas explored in *Mansfield Park* for a "new Romanticism": unlike previous Austen heroines, Anne Elliot marries not the great house (Pemberley, Donwell, or Mansfield/Thornton Lacey) but the wide world itself—in the form of the imperial navy (1987:56–57). Such a reading might recognize the rush of English confidence in the decades following Trafalgar, but Weissman seems to miss the balance of *Persuasion* in her enthusiasm for the novel's all-conquering sailors. Although the Crofts and Wentworths bring new energy to the moribund gentry of Kellynch, the

ending of Austen's last completed novel carefully weighs the freedom and mobility of the new imperial domain against its moral
accountability: "[Anne] gloried in being a sailor's wife, but she
must pay the tax of quick alarm for belonging to that profession
which is, if possible, more distinguished in its domestic virtues
than in its national importance" (253–54). In the last sentence,
Anne does at last find a congenial family, coming to "belong" by
marriage to the imperial navy; the "tax" of sudden alarm, and the
balancing of "domestic virtue" against "national importance" in
the final phrase, however, suggest that this might be a contingent
and incomplete affiliation.

The enlarged social relations of empire extend Anne's new
boundaries far enough to allow her marriage outside the traditional gentry, but no farther. A sense of national mission and
the concept of a sacred domesticity were to become the paired
consolidations of empire in the Victorian period, the moral superiority of English *domestic* life not only vindicating but warrant-
ing and even necessitating its *national* mission abroad.[11] The construction of the navy, the instrument of Britain's imperial success,
as the custodian of "distinguished ... domestic virtues" in *Persuasion* demonstrates the reciprocity between the domestic and
national realms, the one underwriting the continuity of the other.
In Austen's later novels, the increased moral influence of the navy
and its admirers succeeds to the extent that it displaces the im-
provident Walter Elliots or the amoral Crawfords (Mary Crawford's mockery of naval "rears and vices" is censured as a significant moral lapse) from respectable country families. But the attendant sense of Englishness with its nationalist overtones is an
already double-edged attribute for heroines like Anne, Emma, and
even Fanny Price—confining as it affirms, imprisoning as it ex-
pands.

⊥

Where *Persuasion* ends with Sir Walter's reluctant acceptance of
the imperial navy into the old landowning gentry, a few decades
later Gaskell's *North and South* (1853), accepts as given the perfect
eligibility of the naval profession. Like *Mansfield Park*, *North and
South* is interested in the relations between vocation, profession,
and feminine influence; like *Persuasion*, it is concerned with the
incorporation by marriage and moral improvement of yet another

occupation made possible by the progress of empire. Early in the novel the heroine, Margaret Hale, declares her aristocratic and outmoded preferences: "I don't like shoppy people. . . . I like all people whose occupations have to do with the land; I like soldiers and sailors, and the three learned professions, as they call them" (50). By the final chapters, Margaret has learned not only to accept but to champion a category she had earlier dismissed as "shoppy"; in the course of the novel the industrial magnate and merchant-manufacturer are established as England's most recent—and most powerful—"pioneers of civilization" at home and abroad (170).

Read mainly as a record of internal tensions between agricultural South and industrializing North, Gaskell's novel is also very much a product of the midcentury in its consciousness of industrialism's international and imperial role. As Thornton exults to the Hales, who have newly migrated to the manufacturing capital of Darkshire from the New Forest countryside, industrial success has been the agent of far-reaching control: "What great future lay concealed in that rude model of Sir Richard Arkwright's. The rapid development of what might be called a new trade, gave those early masters enormous power . . . *I don't mean merely over the workmen; I mean over purchasers—over the whole world's market*" (124; emphasis added). The true relation between the power of this "new trade" and "the whole world's market" has been outlined by Brooks Adams:

> Plassey was fought in 1757, and probably nothing has ever equalled in rapidity . . . the change which followed. In 1760 the flying shuttle appeared. . . . In 1764 Hargreaves invented the spinning jenny, in 1776 Crompton contrived the mule, in 1785 Cartwright patented the powerloom, and chief of all, in 1768 Watt matured the steam engine. . . . But though these machines served as outlets for the accelerating movement of the time, they did not cause that acceleration. . . . Possibly since the world began, no investment has ever yielded the profit reaped from the Indian plunder.
>
> (Quoted, Mukherjee 1974:398–99)

England's industrial power was possible largely because of imperial conquest and the consequent expansion of capital. Like Dickens' Dombey, Thornton, the manufacturer hero of *North and South,* is a figure of imperial capitalism; like the gallant sailor/adventurer Walter Gay in Dickens' novel, his inspiration is England's heritage of militant mercantilism. Thornton's exalted sense of mission draws on a stock of biblical and historical imagery associated with the glorious imperial power of trade:

> Far away, in the East and in the West, where his person would never be known, his name was to be regarded, and his wishes to be fulfilled, and his word pass like gold. That was the idea of merchant-life with which Mr Thornton had started. "Her merchants be like princes," said his mother, reading the text aloud, as if it were a trumpet-call to invite her boy to the struggle. . . . He sought to possess the influence of a name in foreign countries and faraway seas,—to become the head of a firm that should be known for generations . . . here in his own town, his own factory, among his own people.
>
> (1970b:511)

The prophetic overtones of this passage invest Thornton's manufacturing and trading successes with a moral and even heroic dimension. The resemblance of this language to the glorification of commerce in the eighteenth century suggests that Gaskell (and —to a lesser extent—Dickens, as I show in chapter 3) is drawing on a well-established set of associations from the great age of the merchant/trader to ennoble a new kind of merchant prince.[12] Thornton, for all the real miseries his "new trade" inflicts on England's laboring poor, is figured as his country's new champion abroad, spreading "civilization" and trade side by side. When the mild Mr. Hale reproves Thornton for neglecting the moral improvement of his "hands"—"It strikes me that you might pioneer a little at home. They are a rough heathenish set of fellows, these Milton men of yours" (171)—the nature of the manufacturer's civilizing mission at home and abroad becomes very clear.

If preeminence "far away in the East and in the West" is necessary to Thornton's success "here in his own town, his own factory, among his own people," the relationship implied here indicates something of the complex textual exchange between center and margins I have been trying to outline. As Eric Stokes has noted, the reforming impulse that consolidated conquest into empire in India at the end of the eighteenth century was complexly linked to a profound change at home: "It was a change being wrought in the character of the Englishman at his centre; the product of advancing industrialism, of the ascendancy of the new middle classes, and of the emergence of a new ethic for a new society. . . .

Its influence in English history is too pervasive to be measured by any conventional yardstick. . . . [It was] the moral agency responsible for Victorian 'respectability,' the power which tamed and disciplined the anarchic individualism of the Industrial Revolution. Its connexion with India is particularly intimate" (1959:27–28). This "change wrought in the . . . Englishman at his centre" and its interplay with the outer world, the emergence of a dominant caste whose values combine Thornton's masterful conviction of imperial destiny with the keen moral conscience of the Hales, is very much the interest of *North and South* (as it is also, less obviously, the interest of *Mansfield Park* and *Persuasion*).

Margaret's role, as inheritor of the pastoral benevolence of her father as well as the aristocratic tradition of her mother's family, is to infuse Thornton's brutal relationship with his industrial "hands" with the responsibility a good country squire feels for his tenants —a combination that attempts to legitimate itself by drawing on an eighteenth-century discourse of beneficent commerce and trade represented "as the proper distribution [at home] of the fruits of the earth which had been garnered by Englishmen as honorary lords of the earth" (Kenny 1984:54). Gaskell's attempt to incorporate these characteristics of the good landlord in her updated nineteenth-century merchant-manufacturer, however, depends in turn on the maintenance of a very different model of imperial and international relations.

As Antigua and the West Indies exist on the margins of *Mansfield Park, Persuasion,* and *Sanditon,* enabling, shaping, or transforming the destinies of English country places, Gaskell's divided North and South are bounded by a discernible periphery of "East and West." The subplot of mutiny and exile involving Margaret's sailor brother in this narrative of internal and localized conflict has been characterized as inept and contrived, but such a reading misses Gaskell's parallel structuring of the insular and imperial stories.[13] The sister and brother are characterized by their shared instinct of resistance to the imperial system; Margaret's fierce anger at the individual miseries and injustices of industrialism corresponds to the report of Frederick's rebellion against harsh naval discipline. Frederick is finally driven to lead a mutiny against his brutal captain when a sailor is killed in a meaningless piece of exhibitionism, a reaction paralleling the desperate anger of the rioting "hands" when they hear of Thornton's importation of cheap Irish labor to break their strike.[14]

Within the moral framework suggested in the early chapters of the novel, the mutineers, the striking workers, Fred, and Margaret herself are all motivated by a similar impulse in their individual rebellions: to humanize the huge naval and industrial structures on which England's preeminence depends. In Margaret's discussion with Higgins, the workers' chief spokesman, for example, the strikers are compared to loyal soldiers:

> "I look forward to the chance of dying at my post sooner than yield. That's what folk call fine and honourable in a soldier, and why not in a poor weaver-chap?"
> "But," said Margaret, "a soldier dies in the cause of the Nation—in the cause of others."
> He laughed grimly. "My lass . . . don't yo' think I can keep three people . . . on sixteen shilling a week? Dun yo' think it's for mysel' I'm striking work at this time? Its just as much in the cause of others as yon soldier—only, m'appen, the cause he dies for it's just that of somebody he never clapt eyes on."
>
> (183)

Similarly, the young sailors following Fred's lead against the Captain are convinced it is their duty to resist "tyranny" and "defy arbitrary power" (154).

Each of the opposing sides can claim theirs as "the cause of the Nation." Thornton invokes the authority of vital international trade ("the whole world's market") for his lowering of wages and resort to nonunion Irish labor. At the personal level, Mr. Hale deplores the navy's implacable enmity toward his son, but acknowledges, "It is necessary, of course, for government to take very stringent measures for . . . offences against authority, more particularly in the navy, where a commanding officer needs to be surrounded . . . with . . . all the power there is at home to back him. . . . [Mutiny] is a fresh and vivid crime on the Admiralty books till it is blotted out by blood" (265). Although *North and South* can, unlike *Persuasion,* articulate the "vices" of the admiralty, it must end by acknowledging the "national importance" if not the distinguished "domestic virtues" of that essential overarching system. The imperial framework on which Thornton's industrial and trading success depends ensures that in the end the novel must abandon its effort to find justice for Fred, unable to reconcile his cause with the Admiralty's higher claim to "the cause of the Nation."

Instead, Fred is forced to abandon England—perhaps a necessary and inevitable expatriation given his un-English looks and temperament. If the Milton workers are "rough" and "heathenish" in their ways, Fred is marked by his "swarthiness of complexion" that suggests his "sense of latent passion . . . the instantaneous ferocity of expression that comes over . . . all natives of wild or southern countries" (313). Unable to reconcile himself with the imperial system, Fred goes into happy exile in Spain while his more resolute, indubitably English, sister has a significant role to play in England's lofty destiny.

But if the struggle to humanize the huge system of the admiralty must be reluctantly abandoned, Gaskell's text can find some accommodation in the internal conflict between North and South, because the opposition between Thornton and Margaret has been figured throughout as an erotic and emotional tension. Though the forced nature of this resolution is suggested by the outdated and melodramatic machinery of deceit, misunderstood honor, and coincidence that advances their courtship, in the end, love for Margaret educates Thornton to consider the human claims of his "hands" and appreciate the moral distinctions of the refined South, while Margaret learns in turn to respect the national role of the Northern manufacturer. Their unlikely matchmakers are Higgins, the truculent union man, and Bell, the crusty Oxford don who leaves Margaret an enormous legacy.

In its closing chapters, *North and South* manages to combine its various conflicting groups into some semblance of unity only by recourse to the conventional marriage plot that underwrites, however shakily, the pairing of social and moral opposites. If Gaskell's attempt to couple refined morality with the wealth and power created by empire seems less successful than that of Austen in *Persuasion,* it is partly because the hints of "quick alarm" at the end of the earlier novel can no longer be contained within a single paragraph. The strikes, murders, and mutiny that erupt throughout the narrative of *North and South* suggest the inability of the marriage plot to absorb any longer the contradictions and tensions of imperial and capitalist expansion, a failure that becomes even more marked in the forced domestic relations of *Dombey and Son* and *Edwin Drood* discussed in the following chapters.

৴

The symbolic union of North and South at the end of Gaskell's novel has been condemned not only for the weakness of its marriage plot but also because of its fantasy of Mr. Bell's unexpected legacy that will enable a chastened Thornton to reestablish his bankrupt factory. In *Culture and Society*, Raymond Williams suggests a similarity between Bell's legacy to Margaret and the happy ending of Gaskell's 1848 novel, *Mary Barton*, characterizing both endings as a "going outside" (1983a:95) the circumstances established in the body of the narrative.[15] A "Condition-of-England" novel concerned with the miseries and temptations of industrial Manchester in the hungry forties, *Mary Barton* ends by relocating Mary, her family, and her friends in a prosperous and pastoral Canada. Gillian Beer comments on this "happy ending": "Escape, not transformation, is seen as the only true record of what currently is being performed in society. . . . [Gaskell] doesn't pretend to have solved society, only her novel" (1978:248).

Beer's comments are representative of the body of critical response to the migration solutions in several mid–nineteenth-century texts; readings that perceive migration as a solution at the level of plot, a "literary" rather than a "realistic" attempt to resolve the authentic social difficulties raised in the midsections of the novels. What seems to receive little or no emphasis in such readings is the extent to which literary and plot devices—the "beginnings, turning points, and endings of fiction"—are themselves socially generated rather than neutral or arbitrary ploys. Instead of being read within the same interpretive framework as the rest of the narrative, those concerns that are presented as "a true record of what currently is being performed in society," the migrations and overseas voyages in novels such as *Mary Barton*, *Alton Locke*, *David Copperfield*, and *Great Expectations* are often read within a different frame of reference—one of "magic" or "escape"—rather than as part of the novel's processing and configuration of the specific social situation seen as its main concern.[16]

The earlier sections of this chapter examined the spatial connections between the English places of Austen and Gaskell and a textually constituted map of empire, tracing the relations between the internal and domestic and the national and imperial relations in these novels. The resolution by migration in *Mary Barton* can be read as the ultimate expression of the same spatial relationship; a relationship neither sudden nor unprepared for but based on this existing network of connections, influences, and transactions. Indeed, the rearrangement and repopulation of the places of empire complement the novel's naming and mapping of those places in relation to an English center.

The question of migration is integral to the discourse of empire. According to Alfred Crosby: "In 1800, North America, after almost two centuries of succcesful European colonization . . . had a population of fewer than 5 million whites. . . . Australia had only 10,000, and New Zealand was still Maori country. Then came the deluge. Between 1820 and 1930, well over 50 million Europeans migrated" (1986:5).

European mass migration is a product of the cultural consolidations of empire in the early and mid–nineteenth century, rather than the conquests and settlements of the previous decades. The representation of migration, its formulation in discourse, and its constitution and canvassing in various literary forms during the 1830s and 1840s, thus becomes extremely significant. Although some anti-industrial critics like Cobbett were opposed to such a solution, seeing it as a strategy to further depopulate the countryside by getting rid "not of the idlers, not of the pensioners, not of the dead-weight . . . but [of] *these working people* who are grudged even the miserable morsel that they get" (1985:310), many more commentators address migration as necessary to the maintenance of English society. It figures most frequently as a necessary outlet —a new field of effort, based on Roman or Greek models, for surplus English energies; as a fulfillment of Anglo-Saxon racial destiny; or as a kind of waste pipe to draw off the effluents of civilized society (Bodelson 1960). Edward Bulwer-Lytton's popular 1849 novel *The Caxtons,* for example, incorporates into its narrative a lengthy essay on migration disguised as a letter from a successful politician to an ambitious young man. In *The Caxtons,* the group of men who migrate to Australia in imitation of colonists of classical Greece and Rome includes the disgraced heir of a noble family, the poor but virtuous hero, Pisistratus, and a fierce young Chartist whose leveling principles survive only until he is called to defend this new "Latium" from Aboriginal reprisals.

The period of Chartist unrest was, uncoincidentally, the period when the migration debate was at its most intense. The scheme of privatized "systematic colonization," proposed by Edward Gibbon Wakefield, for example, received an impressive degree of attention and support during the Chartist 1830s and 1840s.[17] Among the more famous proponents of large-scale colonization as a means of dealing with "the Physical-Force Chartist" was Thomas Carlyle; in fact, Carlyle's 1839 essay *Chartism* (which—as Beer also points out—is, like *Mary Barton,* concerned with the narrative difficulties posed by the Chartist movement) ends with an extravagant vision of migration, written in characteristically suggestive language:

> Over population? And yet, if this small Western rim of Europe is overpeopled, does not everywhere else a whole vacant Earth, as it were, call to us, Come and till me, come and reap me! . . . [A] world where Canadian forests stand unfelled, boundless Plains and Prairies unbroken with the plough; and on the west and on the east green desert spaces never yet made white with corn; and to the overcrowded little nook of Europe, our Terrestrial Planet, nine-tenths of it yet vacant or tenanted by nomads, is still crying "come and till me, come and reap me!". . . Is it not as if this swelling, simmering, never-resting Europe of ours stood, once more, on the verge of an expansion without parallel; struggling, struggling like a mighty tree again about to burst in the embrace of summer, and shoot forth broad frondent boughs which would fill the whole earth?
>
> (326–27)

The final scene of *Mary Barton* draws, in almost identical terms, on *Chartism*'s image of a wild fertility profitably managed. Mary and her family are presented by the narrator in their new Canadian settlement: "I see a long low wooden house, with room enough, and to spare. The old primeval trees are felled and gone for many a mile around. . . . There is a garden . . . and far beyond . . . stretches an orchard. The glory of the Indian summer is over all, making the heart leap at the sight of its gorgeous beauty" (465). Mary's husband appears to announce the proposed migration of more of their old friends, including Margaret, the blind folksinger, and their sailor cousin, Will—a reunion signaling the rerooting of the best of the old world in the new. The crucial point about this final scene of reunion and recreation of community in the midst of cultivation and plenty (Mary is singing "daddy comes, \ With his pocket full of plums") is that, like the concluding vision of *Chartism*, it is presented less as a scene of contrast than of *continuity* with the industrial deprivation of the earlier chapters. Similarly, several texts of the "Condition-of-England" school—*Mary Barton, Chartism*, Kingsley's *Alton Locke,* even parts of Disraeli's "Young England" trilogy—find their final solutions by renewing themselves within the boundless expanse of empire.

In *The Road to Botany Bay*, Paul Carter has distinguished the practice of "spatial history" by its engagement with the *process* of exploration, whereas the "kind of history which reduces space to a stage, that pays attention to events unfolding in time alone, might be called imperial history. . . . Rather than focus on the *intentional* world of active, spatial choices, empirical history . . . has as its focus facts which, in a sense, come after the event. The primary object is not to understand or to interpret: it is to legitimate" (1988:xvi). Characteristic of such narratives, Carter continues, is a preference for "fixed and detachable facts, for actual houses, visible clearings and boats at anchor. For these, unlike the intentions which brought them there . . . are durable objects which can be treated as typical, as further evidence of a universal historical process."

Mary Barton's final scene of newly cleared forest occupied by house and orchard draws on this legitimizing imperial narrative and implicitly adopts the Carlylean rationale of historical inevitability. The establishment of nineteenth-century colonial settlements can be seen as "magical" or epic, the stocking or replenishing of a "vacant" earth, only if the material processes of conquest, incorporation, and occupation involved in that operation are disguised or covered over. When the migrations and transportations at the end of Victorian novels are seen as occurring outside their social and discursive contexts, as an arbitrary recourse to "plot" or "textual" solutions or as a kind of geographical *Deus ex machina,* the ideology of Carlyle's green, untenanted deserts seems to do its work almost too well. As both the realities of colonization and their essential relation to a range of causes in England are concealed— a measure of ideological success—migration comes to seem like an impossible external and "literary" solution to the "real" problems it sought to address.

If Carlyle's vision of effortless and natural occupation conceals some of the violent realities of colonial settlement, closer attention suggests that this effect is accomplished largely by the sexualization of his language. The heaving fecundity of a supine earth, the struggle of Europe "like a mighty tree" to "shoot forth broad frondent boughs which would fill the whole earth" deliberately invoke the oppositions of European/Other, virility/passivity and masculine/feminine. The significance of this vocabulary for the simultaneous constitution of gender and empire has been discussed already; it is interesting to note in connection with migration, however, that the expulsion of sexually suspect or compromised women to the unhusbanded territories of empire instantly transforms them into good wives, thus solving not only social "Condition-of-England" problems but also the more complex issue of feminine dissatisfaction.[18] In *Mary Barton,* Mary's "flightiness" is linked repeatedly to that of her beautiful aunt Esther, a "fallen" woman who dies just too soon to join the mass migration to Canada. In *David Copperfield,* heartbroken relatives accompany the compromised Little Emily to Australia, the only possible place for her redemption; Eliot's *Adam Bede* (1859) suggests a similar reformation for the pathetic Hetty Sorrel when her aristocratic lover gets her death sentence commuted to transportation. In *Alton Locke,* a seamstress driven to prostitution declares wistfully, "Oh, if that fine lady as we're making a riding habit for would just spare only half the money that goes on dressing her to send us to the colonies, wouldn't I be an honest girl there?—Maybe even an honest wife!" (91).[19]

The simultaneous moral and environmental transformation effected by the settlement of unsatisfactory or unnecessary women in the fertile but unhusbanded lands of empire, is, I would argue, an extension of the concern over the correct allocation of country property in *Persuasion* or *Mansfield Park.* Just as the moral balance achieved in these texts, like the more precarious reconciliation of *North and South,* establishes Anne Elliot, Fanny Price, and Margaret Hale in their proper places as the—albeit sometimes uneasy— domestic mediators of England's imperial destiny, the ending of *Mary Barton* settles its chastened heroine in the potentially fruitful but improperly wild and unmanaged "wastelands" of Canada. The consolidation, differentiation, and management of space and place become interdependent with the correct positioning of women, a process that subsequently endorses the moral and even metaphysical order of space acted out in novels like *Jane Eyre.*

Beer's final comment on the ending of *Mary Barton* is that it acknowledges its own place, sharing with Carlyle's *Chartism* "a recognition that the text does not occupy the identical amount of space as society" (1978:248). This chapter has tried to show that the organization of certain texts does indeed approximate the arrangement of space and place, if not in "society," then within nineteenth-century discourse. In his reading of place, empire, and inheritance in *Mansfield Park,* Said observes that Fanny Price must learn, as the basis for an English country-house education, to "put the map of Europe together" (1989:155). What is put together in texts like those of Austen and Gaskell discussed here is a cultural map in which empire is fictionally indicated, constituted, annexed, and appropriated.

The epigraph to this chapter quotes from Carter's account of Thomas Livingston Mitchell, surveyor-general of New South Wales between 1827 and 1855. The significance of Mitchell's surveys and reports, Carter maintains, was not their geographical (in)accuracy but their appeal to the colonizing imagination; Mitchell's achievement was that he "invented a country for others to live in" (1988:135). The novels I discuss here both authorize and are authorized by individual maps and histories like Mitchell's; like them, they produce a cultural space, a world for the English imagination to inhabit.

three

🕉

"Wholesale, Retail, and for Exportation": Empire and the Family Business in Dombey and Son

> COMMISSIONERS.—*What articles of trade are best suited to your people, or what would you like brought to your country?*
> OBI.—*Cowries, cloth, muskets, powder, handkerchiefs, coral, beads, hats—anything from the white man's country will please.*
> COMMISSIONERS.—*You are the King of this country, as our Queen is the sovereign of Great Britain; but she does not wish to trade with you; she only desires that her subjects may trade fairly with yours. . . . The Queen of England's subjects would be glad to trade for raw cotton, indigo, ivory, gums, camwood. Now have your people these things to offer in return for English trade goods?*
> OBI.—*Yes.*
> —DICKENS, "THE NIGER EXHIBITION"

*T*HIS UNEQUAL exchange performs, through several filters of official interpretation, the recognizable dynamics of colonial trade. Obi's interlocutors represent one of the best-known trade delegations of the Victorian period, the Niger Expedition—a joint project of the Colonial Office and the Admiralty with the cooperation of abolitionist and missionary interests. The Expedition's aims were, in its own words, "to assist in the abolition of the Slave Trade and further the innocent trade of her Majesty's subjects";

or in the words of Dickens' 1848 review of the Expedition's authorized *Narrative:* "the abolition, in great part, of the Slave Trade, by
means of treaties with native chiefs, to whom were to be explained
the immense advantages of general unrestricted commerce with
Great Britain in lieu thereof" (1913a:46).[1]

The ceremonial dialogue of trade negotiation does not obscure
the power relations implicit in this missionary armada, designed as
it was to awaken Africans "to a sense of their own degradation"
(47). Eric Williams and others have suggested that abolitionist
blockades and trade expeditions in fact prepared the way for the
full-scale colonization of Africa, developing markets for English
products and accumulating information about local conditions in
these exploratory forays (Williams 1972; Cell 1979). Both Dickens
and the official *Narrative* represent the free trade of empire, or
"general unrestricted commerce with Great Britain," as "innocent"
in contrast to the un-English monopoly in slaves attributed to Obi.
Dickens' essay, seven years after the event, however, turns out to
be not a defense of the premises of the Expedition but a violent
repudiation of "the heated visions of philanthropists for the railroad Christianisation of Africa, and the abolition of the Slave
Trade" (62).

By this time, indeed, the Niger Expedition had become a byword of costly failure (46). Bad planning, unsuitable climate,
and African covert resistance (in Dickens' terms, "their climate,
their falsehood, and deceit") had ended in scores of deaths among
the English crew and a cancellation of the entire project. Dickens'
essay thus becomes more than a simple review of the Expedition's
Narrative; it is an occasion to comment on the recent direction
of colonial and trade policy and indirectly on the wider issues of
free trade and empire, domestic ethics and foreign policy, and,
most significant, the source of moral authority over these issues at
home.

This chapter suggests that the debate over imperial policy and
moral authority was also charged with the tensions of contemporary representations of woman's influence. Judith Newton and
others have shown that a domestic sphere of soft, conciliatory
feminine influence was a particularly mid-Victorian creation, formulated as a part of the growing economic and social power of the
middle classes (Newton 1987:124–40; Armstrong 1987:72–74).[2]
Although Bernard Semmel has demonstrated that "the essentially
mercantilist assumptions and objectives embodied in . . . 'classic'

. . . imperialism were far from absent in the thinking [that] erected the system of free trade in the last half of the eighteenth and in the first half of the nineteenth centuries" (1970:5), the doctrine of free trade is usually cast as inherently anti-imperialist.

A key aspect of the mid-Victorian debate over colonial policy was the ostensible pacifism of free trade, often perceived as a softening or feminization of a more assertive expansionism. In the Niger essay, Dickens attributes the misguided humanitarianism of the Expedition to "the weird old women who go about, and exceedingly roundabout, on the Exeter Hall Platform"(45).[3] *Bleak House* (1853) firmly locates feminine moral authority in Esther's housewifely skills, whereas Mrs. Jellyby's exercise of "telescopic philanthropy," in the Borrioboola Gha project (another experimental settlement on the banks of the Niger) leads directly to household mismanagement and anarchy.[4] The usurpation of the masculine platforms of economy and colonial policy by "weird old women" (both politicized women and men feminized by humanitarianism) simultaneously perverts the ideology of gendered spheres of influence at home and guarantees disaster abroad.

The text I want to situate in relation to a discourse of empire, trade, and feminine moral authority is, however, not *Bleak House* but *Dombey and Son*, a novel usually discussed for its treatment of the local effects of mid-Victorian capitalism. *Dealings with the Firm of Dombey and Son: Wholesale, Retail and for Exportation*, is, as the repressed second half of the title makes clear, Dickens' parable of mercantile capitalism; it is also inherently and immediately a narrative predicated on an economy of empire.[5] The passage locating the house of Dombey against the key institutions of metropolitan power maps this fundamental connection:

> Though the offices of Dombey and Son were within the liberties of the City of London . . . yet were there hints of adventurous and romantic story to be obtained in some of the adjacent objects. . . . The Royal Exchange was close at hand; the Bank of England, with its vaults of gold and silver "down among the dead men" underground, was their magnificent neighbour. Just around the corner stood the rich East India House, teeming with suggestions of precious stuffs and stones, tigers, elephants, howdahs, hookahs, umbrellas, palm trees, palanquins, and gorgeous princes of a brown complexion . . . with their slippers very much turned up at the toes. Anywhere in the immediate vicinity there might be seen pictures of ships speeding away full sail to all parts of the world; outfitting

warehouses ready to pack off anybody anywhere, fully equipped in half an hour; and little timber midshipmen in obsolete naval uniforms, eternally employed outside the shop doors of nautical Instrument-makers.

(1970:87–88)

Here, empire not only supplies the obvious link between the separated "money world" and "water world" previous critics have discerned in the novel; it activates capitalist expansion, generating ships, outfitting warehouses, and producing scientific instruments.[6] The financial institutions of the Bank, Royal Exchange, and the House of Dombey combine the power of an empire represented by neighboring East India House, translating the stuff of oriental romance directly into the substance of metropolitan wealth, and converting the interior of the Bank of England to subterranean coffers of piratical gold.[7]

Dickens' cartography locates the novel's opposing forces, the House of Dombey and the Wooden Midshipman's shop—the one signifying money and destructive pride, the other romance and childlike love—on the meeting ground of the East India Docks. But how is the textual promise of "romantic and adventurous story" here separable from the grim moral of capitalist expansion interrogated in Dombey's career? The doctrine of empire represented in East India House encompasses the spirit of romance and adventure that enraptures Walter Gay and his quixotic naval guardians, Uncle Sol and Captain Cuttle. At the same time, empire is the incontrovertible image of Dombey's solipsism: "The earth was made for Dombey and Son to trade in, and the sun and moon were made to give them light. Rivers and seas were formed to float their ships . . . winds blew for or against their enterprises; stars and planets circled in their orbits, to preserve inviolate a system of which they were the centre" (50).

A cosmic system with imperial trade at its center is also the subject of Thackeray's *The Newcomes.* Published in 1853, about five years after *Dombey and Son,* this novel traces the career of a banking family from its beginnings in the dissenting circles of Clapham to its present-day decadence and corruption. The novel's central figures are the incurably romantic and youthful Colonel Newcome and his much-indulged son, Clive (named for the military hero of Plassey). After retiring his commission in India, the colonel becomes embroiled in the fraudulent dealings of the Bundlecund

Bank, a vast multinational with correspondents in "Sydney, Singapore, Canton, and of course, London":

> With China they did an immense opium trade, of which the profits were so great, that it was only in private sittings of the B. B. managing committee that the details . . . of these operations could be brought forward. . . . The orders from Birmingham for idols alone (made with their copper and paid in their wool) were enough to make the low church party in England cry out; and a debate upon this subject actually took place in the House of Commons, of which the effect was to send up the shares very considerably upon the London exchange.
>
> (1868, 2:129)

Colonel Newcome's constitutional innocence is damaged as he becomes, progressively, a board member of the bank, a Member of Parliament, and a candidate for directorship of the East India Company. As in Dickens' novel, marriage is a function of the economy; both Clive and his cousin Ethel are sacrificed to mercenary alliances. The colonel's redemption is possible only after the bank, like Dombey's grandiose ventures, overreaches itself, causing bankruptcy and ruin throughout the empire.[8]

In its record of the adventurous and romantic frontier soldier corrupted by metropolitan mercantilism, Thackeray's novel, like Dickens', participates in contradictory discourses of expansion. If the imperial enterprise is implicitly sanctioned in *Dombey and Son* by the romance attached to seafaring, its counterpart in *The Newcomes* is the heroic status of the army, represented in Orme's classic history of English conquest in India. The colonel's prized edition of this military text is evoked several times in the novel and serves as the agent of his final rescue. In both novels, *colonial* expansion is romanticized, even as its agent, the expansion of capital, is decried for its metropolitan consequences: the emotional bankruptcies and recurring financial crises so characteristic of mid-Victorian capitalism in novels like *Little Dorrit, Cranford,* and *Martin Chuzzlewit.*

In *The Ideology of Adventure,* Michael Nerlich discusses the collaboration of merchant capital and state force in early voyages of exploration, and points out that "the Crown, merchant adventurers, and explorer or conqueror adventurers" (1987:129) combined in the appropriation of England's earliest colonies. The fundamental connection between mercantile capital and colonial enterprise is encapsulated in the twin meanings of "adventure": "both the exploration with its risks and the (risky) business venture" (128).[9] By the early nineteenth century, the growth of industrial capital and the hunt for foreign markets had brought the older mercantile monopolies into conflict with the new orthodoxy of free trade. That classic monopolist enterprise, the East India Company, was to be dismantled after the uprising of 1857, signifying, Ramkrishna Mukherjee (1974) has shown, the movement of capital from its overtly expansionist mercantile phase to the free trade strategies of triumphant industrialism.[10] In the usage of both Dickens and Thackeray, the tensions between old-style mercantilism and free trade are felt as a dislocation between the hitherto linked concepts of capital, colonization, and adventure: the "hints of adventurous and romantic story" are transferred, apparently unquestioned, to the colonial margins, while the operations of capital are visible only in their social and human costs at home. Most often, this cost is measured in its impact on family and sexual relations, as a trading institution becomes The House, and domestic subjects—women and children—are commodified within the mercantile economy.

Such a displacement of mercantilism's impact might account for the tendency to structure these novels as a series of oppositions: feminine/masculine, nature/progress, love/capitalism. In *Dombey and Son,* this polarization, based on the conflict between Florence and Dombey, is most often characterized by a symbolism of the sea as natural, fluid, and cyclical as opposed to the rigid industrial realities of man-made progress. But as David Musselwhite points out, a "structural description of the polarities of the book . . . is no more than a practice of collusion with the very ambition the text sets itself—that of distracting attention away from its real conditions of existence . . . and promoting a 'critical' discourse ever preempted by its object" (1978:211).

The incorporation of the hitherto unconsidered factor of empire problematizes the binary opposition between "money world" and "water world," revealing the ocean as much an agent of trade and capital in the text, as is the metropolis, disrupted and fragmented by an eruption of railroads.[11] The prevailing view of the ocean as a privileged symbol of the feminine in *Dombey and Son* is best expressed by Auerbach:

> Florence's realm, the sea, exists independent of the mechanized products of civilization. . . . Like the ebb and flow of the female

cycle . . . its rhythms are involuntary and unconscious, related to the flow of emotion and dream; lacking a destination to shape its movements, it has all the interminable attraction of a world without end. Unlike the railroad's shriek, its voice is quiet and its language is private. . . . The mindlessness of its repeated motions reminds us of Florence's incessant returns to the unyielding breast of her father until it melts for her. Her persistence seems more plausible in geological than in psychological terms . . . her movements are as involuntary and unwilled as the sea's are. Her kinship with the sea is appropriate to her role as vessel of woman's influence.

(1985:117)

But the sea and Florence's femininity are less eternal and immutable in their operations than they are socially and ideologically constituted agents. In Newton's essay on the formulation of a mid-Victorian ideal of womanhood, "the awful inevitability of Florence" reveals "the hold of the ideology of woman's influence" on Dickens as well as Dombey—a hold Newton demystifies in her nuanced materialist analysis (1987:133). Similarly, the ocean in *Dombey and Son* can be read as an eternal reservoir of natural "femininity" only if we exclude its more evident operation as a means of global traffic and imperial wealth.[12] All the sympathetic characters of the novel undertake colonial voyages to named destinations in order to perform specific tasks necessary to the profitable maintenance of empire: Walter and Florence embark on a trading voyage to a China forcibly opened to England's opium trade; Dombey sends Walter aboard the prophetically named "Son and Heir" to act as a junior clerk in his factory in Barbados; Uncle Sol uses his scientific skills to work his way as a seaman from Demerara to China in search of his missing nephew.

Gender and trade seem, rather, to be organized as linked operations of a mercantile economy, with Florence's unrelenting and seemingly immutable "femininity" as much a construct of that system as Dombey's capitalist imperiousness.[13] In place of an oppositional structure of masculine/feminine or ocean/railroad, *Dombey and Son* is examined here as a complex interchange between the key categories of capital and adventure or "romance," each implicated and enmeshed in the overarching ideology of empire. Crucial to this argument is the interplay between the continually evolving discourses that constituted and managed both gender and empire. The *Narrative* of the Niger Expedition, Dickens' critique, *The Newcomes,* and *Dombey and Son* all employ a vocabulary of private and public, domestic and foreign, to participate in a discourse of trade and empire that simultaneously addresses the "local" issues of home, family, and woman's influence.

ᴣᓂ

> COMMISSIONERS.—*Is there any road from Aboh to Benin?*
> OBI.—*Yes.*
> COMMISSIONERS.—*They must all be open to the English.*
> OBI.—*Yes.*
> COMMISSIONERS.—*All the roads in England are open alike to all foreigners. . . . Will Obi let the English build, cultivate, buy and sell without annoyance?*
> OBI.—*Certainly.*
> COMMISSIONERS.—*If your people do wrong to them, will you punish them?*
> OBI.—*They shall be judged, and if guilty, punished.*
> COMMISSIONERS.—*When the English do wrong, Obi must send word to an English officer. . . . You must not punish white people.*
> OBI.—*I assent to this. (He now became restless and impatient).*
>   —DICKENS, "THE NIGER EXPEDITION"

In 1855, a Victorian bureaucrat, Sir John Bowrigg, felt confident enough to declare: "Free Trade is Jesus Christ and Jesus Christ is Free Trade" (quoted, Anderson 1990:34–35). As early as 1833, Harriet Martineau had attacked the East India Company's practices in Ceylon in "Cinnamon and Pearls," a tale aimed at proving that the "evil spirit of monopoly" (77) had perverted the true ends of colonization. In the mid-1840s, the height of the free-trade controversy, *Dombey and Son* is much more ambiguous in its attitude to the honorable Company. Details of the free trade debates trouble Dickens' text, however, as Paul's dancing master is obsessed by the particular mystery: "What you were to do with your raw materials, when they came into your ports in return for your drain of gold[?] . . . Sir Barnet Skettles had much to say . . . but it did not appear to solve the question, for Mr Baps retorted, Yes, but supposing Russia stepped in with her tallows; which struck Sir Barnet almost dumb, for he could . . . only say, Why, then you must fall back upon your cottons, he supposed" (270).[14]

Despite the supposed pacifism of free trade ideology, "the free trade era was the great age of colonization and colonial trade" (Semmel 1970:8). Colonial policy worked to ensure that more and more trade routes were "open to the English." During the mid–nineteenth century, an aggressive free trade policy resulted in two Opium Wars when Chinese ports were besieged to ensure the free trade of England's narcotics, while in India a series of "annexations" were carried out along the northwestern frontier as a supposed protection against Russia, the rising trade rival so feared by Mr. Baps. Compared with these military incursions, and the overt expansionism of earlier and later stages in English history, the Niger Expedition reflects the combination of humanitarian and abolitionist interests that ultimately reinforced the interests of an intensified and more violent imperialism.[15]

The intimate connection between the reformist impulses of the Niger Expedition and a strain of the new free trade capitalism is apparent in the founder of Thackeray's banking dynasty, the formidable matriarch, Sophia Newcome, whose duties seem to her a perfectly consistent blend of the financially and spiritually profitable: "To manage the great House of Hobson Brothers and Newcome; to attend to the interests of the enslaved negro, to awaken the benighted Hottentot . . . to listen untired on her knees after a long day's labour . . . all these things had this woman to do and she fought her fight womanfully: imperious but deserving to rule" (1:18).[16] Dickens' extreme hostility to this combination is evident in his attack on philanthropic and missionary interests and "the weird old women" who supported the Niger project. His attack on the Niger Expedition and the expansionist and adventurous vision of imperial trade interrogated in *Dombey and Son* can be read, in this context, as complementary contributions to the free trade debates of the period. This section considers the workings of these debates over trade and empire, adventure and quietism, and their impact on the domestic concerns of home, family, and woman's influence, through the personal transactions often seen as the primary "Dealings" of *Dombey and Son*.

Partners with greater and lesser stakes in the imperial connection people *Dombey and Son*, beginning with the "black cook in a black caboose" serving on Walter's ship and the ferocious little Bill Blitherstone, one of a long line of unfortunate children returned "home" from India to acquire a metropolitan education (342). The greatest of these partners is Dombey himself, the embodiment of old-style mercantilism: "a pecuniary Duke of York," (58) "paramount in the greatest city in the universe" (362), with "a name . . . that is known and honoured in the British possessions abroad" (188). The eighteenth century was the great age of the merchant prince in literature, as the "agent of commerce [the merchant] was also celebrated as the agent of progress and civilisation, the embodiment of civilised standards derived from his commercial experience" (Dabydeen 1985:32). Still, Dabydeen adds, the merchant prince was, almost from the beginning, also a compromised and suspect figure, tainted by profits from the slave trade and bloodshed in the colonies.

In Dickens' nineteenth-century merchant prince, these relations between profit at home and exploitation abroad, affluence and excess, wealth and violence, emerge somewhat less directly. Blitherstone is the means of the Dombeys' introduction to Major Bagstock, a soldier of "Imperial complexion" (346) who "did all sorts of things . . . with every description of firearm . . . in the East and West Indies" (191).[17] A buffoonish and grotesque figure, the major is at the same time Dombey's surrogate and psychological counterpart, his true "second" in the proposed duel, reflecting at their most extreme the other's self-aggrandizement and aggression. The connection between the two men is most evident in the major's absolute possession of the ultimate imperial commodity, a speechless "dark servant . . . Miss Tox was quite content to classify as a 'native' without connecting him with any geographical idea whatever" (144). An inhabitant of the anonymous outlands of empire, "the Native," who is "currently believed to be a prince in his own country" (350), is himself nameless, answering to "any vituperative epithet" (346) Bagstock might choose for him. Nor is "the Native" ever heard to speak; his only function in the text is to serve the major and receive his gratuitous abuse.

In the accumulation-ridden society of *Dombey and Son*, the function of Bagstock's speechless attendant is an obvious one. Raymond Williams has commented on the problem of representing colonial wealth in literature: "[Austen's] eye for a house, for timber, for the details of improvement, is quick, accurate, monetary. Yet money of other kinds, from the trading houses, from the colonial plantations, has no visual equivalent; it has to be converted to these signs of order to be recognised at all" (1973:115). While "improvement," in all its moral and material connotations, is an indicator of colonial success in novels like *Mansfield Park* and *Per-*

suasion, a different aesthetic tradition relies on the artifacts and objects of empire as a convenient means of reproducing colonial wealth and power. This practice, derived from portraiture and commercial art, frequently employed dark-skinned servants either as emblems of their masters' status or as icons of commercial prosperity.[18] In his commentary on Hogarth's group portrait, *The Wollaston Family,* Dabydeen points out that the dark servant is "a mute, background figure," "a blob of black paint" represented in the portrait only as a token of his employers' "affluence and colonial business interests, not in his own right: among the sitters are a daughter of a Bank of England Director, a Portugal Merchant and Director of the Royal Exchange Assurance, and a future South Sea Company Director and Governor of Virginia" (1987:21). In *Dombey and Son,* almost as richly peopled with the master figures of empire, the shadowy and speechless "Native" again serves as an embodiment of imperial power and control. At the same time, as surely as Dombey's collection of plate in a society where power is expressed through the possession of objects, Bagstock's "delicate exotic" (495) registers his possessor's rating on the scale of economic value.

A second prime indicator on this same scale of luxury and power is female beauty. Introduced to the aristocratic Edith by Bagstock, Dombey hastily acquires her, then loses no time in displaying his bargain to a guest list of "sundry eastern magnates"; his first signs of dissatisfaction with his wife appear when she is not sufficiently enthusiastic in her reception of an East India Company Director (593–94). In refusing to perform for the assembled bankers and magnates, Edith rejects her chief function in the contract between the couple—a bargain understood well enough by both parties. Edith's beauty has always been recognized as a commodity by her mother, the ancient Cleopatra, who has devoted her "pains and labour" (514) to developing it for a future consumer. In this, she is most fundamentally connected to "good Mrs Brown," who makes "a sort of property" of her own daughter, Alice (847), then trades her, on less advantageous terms, to the villainous Carker. Alice bitterly appraises the cost to herself of her own good looks: "There was a girl called Alice Marwood. She was handsome. . . . She was too well cared for, too well trained. . . . What came to that girl comes to thousands every year. It was only ruin and she was born to it . . . There was a criminal called Alice Marwood. . . . And lord, how the gentlemen in court talked about it! and how grave the judge was . . . on her having perverted the gifts of nature—as if he didn't know better than anybody there, that they had been made curses to her!" (570–71).

Alice and Edith are fatally linked by the unnatural transformation of personal gifts into salable goods; a link underscored by their hidden blood relationship and by their common seducer. Here, as elsewhere in Dickens, the location of a range of vices in the same character works to identify a deeper connection. The licentious Carker, agent of public "ruin" for both Alice and Edith, is simultaneously Dombey's trusted agent, speculating in women even as he directs the firm's "prodigious ventures" through "the great labyrinth" of empire (843). Similarly, if Edith must be "sold as infamously as any woman with a halter round her neck is sold" (857), her logical purchaser is that "Colossus of Commerce" (440), Dombey himself. Dombey's desire to "swell the reputation of the House . . . and to exhibit it in magnificent contrast to other merchants' Houses . . . in most parts of the world" (843) is complemented by an imperious insistence on Edith's public recognition of his power: "I must have a positive show and confession of deference before the world, Madam" (652).[19] Trade and sex operate as the medium of exchange in the struggle for control between master and man: Dombey uses Carker as a menial go-between to deliver lordly reprimands to Edith; Carker successfully manipulates the inordinate expansion of Dombey's pride to comprehend both a financial and a sexual downfall. The middle section of the novel is a lengthy scuffle for turf between employer and assistant as Dombey's overweening need for self-assertion (what Auerbach terms his "inveterate phallicism" [1985:112]) is countered by Carker's public embezzlement of the House's funds and subsequent elopement with Dombey's wife.

In this complex interplay of class, sex, and trade, Florence's status is defined by her position as Dombey's daughter. Dombey's fatal error in the novel is his early miscalculation of Florence's worth: "But what was a girl to Dombey and Son! In the Capital of the House's name and dignity, such a child was merely a piece of base coin that couldn't be invested—a bad Boy—nothing more" (51). Such an error in reckoning marks not only a personal but a crucial business failure. Dombey's mistaken assessment of Florence is recalled again in the last pages of the novel: " 'And so Dombey and Son . . .' said Miss Tox, winding up a host of recollections, 'is indeed a daughter, Polly, after all.' 'And a good one!' exclaimed Polly" (941).

The process of Dombey and Son's conversion, its movement from rejecting a bad Boy to accepting a good daughter, involves the recognition and incorporation of feminine influence as a distinct function in the mercantile economy.[20] When Dombey writes Florence off as a bad investment prospect, he misses a factor equally well understood by the designing Carker as by the romantic Captain Cuttle. Both the Captain and Uncle Sol allude to the economic opportunity manifested in Florence on the very first day of Walter's employment by Dombey and Son: "We'll finish the bottle to the House . . . Walter's House. Why it may be his House one of these days, in part. Who knows? Sir Richard Whittington married his master's daughter" (99).

Dombey's refusal to accommodate Florence within the economy of the family business equally denies her a role in the *domestic* economy. As several critics have pointed out, Dombey's angry rejection of that comforting Victorian construct, a de-sexed, nurturing daughter, or "little mother," brings the forbidden possibilities of the father-daughter connection into full focus (Clark 1984; Zwinger 1985).[21] These possibilities include not only dangerous sexuality but domestic rebellion. Left unmanaged or uninvested by paternal authority, womanly influence threatens the patriarchal household. Dombey's resentful suspicion of Florence's influence on her mother, on Paul, and finally and most decisively on Edith (all figures who resist his greatness), turns Florence into Dombey's domestic *rival*, appropriating the devotion due to the husband and father figure: "Who was it who could win his wife as she had won his boy? . . . Who was it whose least word did what his utmost means could not? Who was it who, unaided by his love, regard or notice . . . thrived and grew beautiful when those so aided died?" (648).

Set in opposition to each other, Dombey and Florence become mutually destructive: his hate blighting her life, her love blighting the objects of his life. The reconciliation of the two is effected only by the overthrow of Dombey's unsound economic principles; his bankruptcy, not the blow to his sexual pride, finally undermines and exposes him to Florence's softening influence. Simultaneously, Florence's dangerously unregulated emotion is defused as she is reabsorbed, through marriage and motherhood, into the domestic order. The original family is reconstituted through Florence's union with her childhood "brother," Walter, and by the birth of her son, a second little Paul.[22]

In turn, Florence's containment in marriage signals the regeneration of the family business, a regeneration all the more significant in the economy of the novel for beginning with a trading voyage. Raymond Williams describes Dickens' evasion of a tragic ending for *Dombey and Son* as an act of "willed and moral intervention," a "personal change" in Dombey rectifying the pride of the system: "Kindness and capitalism—a small firm, humbly remembering its origins—are made compatible after all" (1970b:30). The system is certainly amended in the last chapters of the novel but, I would suggest, less by a personal redemption than by a forced realignment of the mercantile ideal with marriage and adventure. It is no coincidence that Florence, probably the first Victorian heroine to sail on a trading venture to China for her honeymoon, gives birth at sea to a son who will be the means by which "from his daughter, after all, another Dombey and Son will . . . rise triumphant" (974).

The system is finally sanctioned in *Dombey and Son,* not through a penitential myth of humble origins, but by the triumphal myth of mercantilism frequently invoked by Walter's friends: that of the legendary Mayor of London, Dick Whittington, who grew rich by venturing his sole possession, his cat, on a trading voyage to Barbary and at the end married his master's daughter. By revivifying this patron saint of London merchants, who united the occupations of apprentice, trader/adventurer, and prosperous city father in a single career, the novel accomplishes a willed reversion to the traditional partnership of commerce and "adventure."[23] The return of Florence and Walter from their successful venture precedes an almost universal restoration of trade and good fortune: "some of our lost ships, freighted with gold . . . come home, truly" (974), bringing in, like Whittington's cat, the foundation of future prosperity and reconciling the old adventurousness of imperial trade with the stability of the mid-Victorian family.

The reconstituted family also forms the base from which a new "Edifice . . . perhaps to equal, perhaps excel" the old House of Dombey is to rise, presided over, in time, by Florence's son. In the revised scheme of things, the benign incorporation of "woman's influence" ensures that the functions of love, marriage, and family are firmly regulated by the exigencies of sound business. Even as the principle of masculine preeminence is temporarily overset, the system is maintained by the continued division of labor by gender. Where the matriarchal Mrs. Newcome's rigid vision of imperial and domestic responsibility is partially redeemed by a posthumous legacy of reconciliation, the ultimate restitution of the reformed patriarch Dombey is neither communal nor public; enfolded in a loving family, he learns to value the second "little Florence" only by "hoard[ing] her in his heart" (975).

꒐

> *The Commissioners requested Mr Schön, the respected missionary, to state to king Obi, in a concise manner, the difference between the Christian religion and heathenism,* together with some description of the settlement at Sierra Leone.
> MR SCHÖN.—*There is but one God.*
> OBI.—*I always understood there were two.*
> —DICKENS, "THE NIGER EXPEDITION"

As the new domesticity makes possible the rise of a more profitably organized Dombey and Son, it rejuvenates the dormant, all-male concern of the Wooden Midshipman. The Midshipman now comes into his own: "instead of being behind the time in some respects . . . he was in truth, a little before it, and had to wait the fullness of the time and the design. . . . The Captain is as satisfied of the Midshipman's importance to the commerce and navigation of his country, as he could possibly be, if no ship left the Port of London without the Midshipman's assistance" (971–72). The happy marriage of "commerce and navigation," capital and science, seems to promise a new flourishing of imperial trade and activity "in the fullness of the time and the design."

The assumption of ever greater imperial progress, however, cannot free itself from its own internal contradictions. The untroubled narrative of imperial prosperity founded on a hard-won domestic stability is implicitly challenged throughout the text by incomplete subplots of revenge and return and through unassimilable rhetorical interjections of disaster and retribution.

The mythologizing of the ocean in *Dombey and Son* draws not only on the legends of Whittington and his fellow adventurers but also on the contemporary literature of naval adventure popularized by Captain Marryat and his imitators in the 1830s and 1840s. Marryat's influence is, of course, visible in the sea stories of Conrad at the end of the century, but its contemporary impact may also be traced in the increasing importance of sailors in novels such as *Mary Barton, North and South, Dombey and Son,* and *Edwin Drood. Westward Ho!* (1855), Charles Kingsley's grandiose recreation of the glory days of Raleigh and Drake, is another, though extreme, example of the mid-Victorian romanticization of the navy. In *Dombey and Son,* however, this mythologizing of the ocean operates also at a more disquieting level, subliminally undercutting the message of the Midshipman's gold-freighted ships. Primary cause of England's imperial mastery and scene of adventurous and ambitious enterprises, the sea is an inescapable source of violence. The unacknowledged story of imperial trade is recalled in the career of the "wonderful madeira" ("which has been to the East Indies and back, I'm not able to say how often" [95]) repeated in a kind of liturgic chorus by Walter and Uncle Sol:

> "Then, there were five hundred casks of such wine aboard; and all hands . . . going to work to stave the casks, got drunk and died drunk, singing 'Rule Britannia' when she settled and went down, and ended with one awful scream in chorus."
>
> "But when the George the Second drove ashore, Uncle . . . the horses breaking loose down below . . . and trampling each other to death . . . set up such human cries, that the crew believing the ship to be full of devils . . . losing heart and head, went overboard in despair. . . ."
>
> "And when," said old Sol, "when the Polyphemous—"
>
> "Private West India Trader, burden three hundred and fifty tons . . ."
>
> "The same," said Sol, "when she took fire, four days' sail with a fair wind out of Jamaica Harbour—"
>
> (95–96)

This compulsive recitation of mysterious naval disasters, accompanied by frantic "Rule Britannias" and inhuman screams, recalls the human cost of empire's "prodigious ventures." Neither resource of buried elemental consciousness nor innocent agent of expansion, this ocean is as compromised by human activity as are the slum dwellings of the metropolis.

A similar image of disaster and contaminated naval adventure occurs in one of the best-known passages in *Dombey and Son,* the lengthy interpolation of an anonymous voice exhorting "unnatural humanity" to repentance. Reminiscent of an apocalyptic sermon, the voice calls on "a good spirit" to reintegrate the human family by stripping away the callous facade of Victorian hypocrisy: "Then should we see how the same poisoned fountains that flow into our hospitals and lazar houses, inundate the jails, and *make the convict ships swim deep, and roll across the seas, and overrun vast continents with crime.* Then should we stand appalled to know that where we generate disease to strike our children down . . . there also we breed, by the same certain process, infancy that knows no innocence, youth without modesty, . . . blasted old age that is a scandal on the form we bear" (738; emphasis added). The force of such a revelation, the passage concludes, *must* transform earthly relations, uniting the human family "like creatures of one common origin, owing *one duty to the Father of one family, and tending to one common end,* to make the world a better place" (738–39; emphasis added).

Like the choric incantation of naval disasters, this passage breaks through the controlling narrative of an achieved domestic stability. If the central story of Florence, Paul/Walter, and Dombey manages to reinstitute a single patriarchal authority by profitably incorporating woman's influence within the family business, the text's marginal stories suggest the problematic nature of that project. Such a model, embodying as it does the profitable virtues of sound investment, collective family duties, and complementary spheres of influence leaves little room for the "unnecessary" or "unattached" members of the community.

Inscribed in the passage's broader polemic of revelation and retribution is Alice Marwood's story. Convict ships, as well as gold- and opium-freighted ships, roll across the seas; each alike brings returns. As inexorably as the avenging fever of *Bleak House,* the transported Alice returns to haunt the metropolis that engendered her "crime." It is no coincidence that *The Newcomes* also features an Alice Marwood character, the unfortunate "factory girl" seduced by the colonel's mercenary nephew, Barnes Newcome. Barnes, who unites elements of both Dombey and Carker, is a master of finance, very "strong in Leadenhall Street" (1:77).[24] His marriage, like Dombey's, results in his wife's elopement; the nameless woman he has seduced dies. The only script projected for his illegitimate children is their transportation, as felons, "by a grateful nation to New South Wales" (2:192). In both novels, the "prodigious venture" of metropolitan capitalism has its cost in unsought returns. These unsolicited returns serve as variations on the questions of succession and inheritance canvassed by Dickens and Thackeray. Mercantile and family dynasties—the Houses of Dombey and of Newcome—generate twin inheritances: the improved, healthy, and venturesome stock represented in Florence and Walter and their children and—less evident—the illicit human traffic of capital and empire.

Alice's story (and its parallel, the "reverse *Maid's Tragedy*" of Edith's transgression and revenge) has a doubly unsettling function in *Dombey and Son*.[25] As the disclosures of illegitimacy and female "ruin" disturb the narrative of "one family" united under a single patriarchal authority, the threatening symmetry of Alice's transportation, return, and retribution interrupts the one-directional flow of the unnatural imperial relationship. If Paul Dombey's dying questions about what the sea brings back pose the "metaphysical" concerns of life and death discussed by some critics, Alice's occluded story of punitive return suggests other possible answers.[26] Such marginal stories of transportation and return are frequently buried in the multiplicity of nineteenth-century novels; enfolded in them are the repressed anxieties of empire. In *Pendennis,* the companion volume to *The Newcomes,* for example, the corrupt Blanche Amory is the daughter of a transported convict who returns to England to blackmail the family. The best example in Dickens' canon is Magwitch's resurrection from the unquiet grave of Australia in *Great Expectations,* a return that ends by implicating and incriminating every institution of the metropolis.[27] The consequences of Alice's return in *Dombey and Son* are far less sweeping. Her anger ensures Carker's death but falls short of a more comprehensive indictment, as the "fallen woman" is provisionally reabsorbed into society through penitence and sickness, then removed permanently by death.[28] But although the vision of *Dombey and Son* is, in this respect, more determinedly benign than that of Dickens' later work, the stories of Edith and Alice, hardened aristocrat and hapless underclass felon, are unassimilable in the narrative of the mutually sustaining, self-contained, middle-class family unit. Similarly, the undirected outlaw energies of the miserable Rob the Grinder ultimately diminish the snug prosperity achieved through the erasure of domestic and class tensions among the Dombeys, Toodleses, and Tootses.

If transportation, revenge, and return suggest a disturbing reversal of the current of "adventurous and romantic story" in *Dombey and Son,* the glorious vision of imperial trade was also being challenged in other directions. The Niger Expedition, for all its humane considerations a pursuit of "general unrestricted commerce with Great Britain," brought grim returns indeed—the futile, miserable, and inexplicable deaths of many of its English participants. (Temperley 1972:58–60). Dickens' indictment of the Expedition, I have said, is much more an attack on the reformist and humanitarian strain in free trade ideology than a petition for quietism and withdrawal from empire. *Bleak House* suggests a buried anxiety that such efforts may be connected to a challenge to masculine authority at home: the domestic disruptiveness of Mrs. Jellyby's Borrioboola Gha project is explicitly linked with Miss Wisk's feminist attack on the "mean . . . domestic mission" of women in the same text, and both causes are contrasted unfavorably with Esther's absorbing interest in her housekeeping keys (375). But if *Bleak House* and the Niger essay are both unremittingly hostile to a more modest and pacific imperial policy, the triumphant regeneration of expansionist mercantilism in *Dombey and Son* cannot dismiss the costly returns of empire, even as it labors to reenact the outdated Whittington legend. The Niger essay ends with an exhortation that sounds dangerously like a retreat: "To your tents, O Israel, but see they are your own tents!" (63). The charged territory of home becomes, in all three texts, both refuge and battleground—a site threatened as well as protected by the operations of unregulated imperial trade and unprincipled domestic adventure.

four

🦋

"Fit Only for a Seraglio": The Discourse of Oriental Misogyny in Jane Eyre *and* Vanity Fair

*T*HIS CHAPTER is concerned with the presentation of feminist interests, in formative nineteenth-century texts, through a model of oppressed oriental womanhood. The title phrase, from Wollstonecraft's introduction to her signal work, *Vindication of the Rights of Woman* (1792), isolates an early instance of a characteristic discursive maneuver: in a single gesture, Wollstonecraft castigates humanism (represented throughout her text by Rousseau and the "Mahometan" creations of Milton) by metaphorically equating its treatment of Western women with the oriental seraglio while she simultaneously participates in its orientalist constructions and exclusions (1982:83).[1] Contained within Wollstonecraft's phrase are the contradictory impulses intersecting in a certain discourse of Western feminism, as the vocabulary of oriental misogyny—fed by a Victorian ideology of empire and informed by feminism's profound ambivalence to Romanticism and Exoticism—becomes an invisible component of feminist representations in a range of narrative forms.[2]

The problematic nature of this identification is evident in a passage from *Jane Eyre,* a text defined by the confrontation of feminist, imperialist, and individualist impulses. The seraglio is the acknowledged referent in the erotic and power play between

Jane and Rochester, as Jane parries her master's "Sultan"-like munificence with her "needle of repartee" during their uneasy courtship:

> He chuckled; he rubbed his hands, "Oh, it is rich to see and hear her!" he exclaimed. . . . I would not exchange this one little English girl for the grand Turk's whole seraglio—gazelle-eyes, houri forms, and all!"
>
> The Eastern allusion bit me again. "I'll not stand you an inch in the stead of a seraglio," I said; "so don't consider me an equivalent for one. If you have a fancy for anything in that line, away with you, sir, to the bazaars of Stamboul, without delay, and lay out in extensive slave-purchases some of that spare cash. . . ."
>
> "And what will you do, Janet, while I am bargaining for so many tons of flesh and such an assortment of black eyes?"
>
> "I'll be preparing myself to go out as a missionary to preach liberty to them that are enslaved. . . . I'll get admitted there, and I'll stir up mutiny; and you, three-tailed bashaw as you are, sir, shall in a trice find yourself fettered amongst our hands: nor will I . . . consent to cut your bonds till you have signed a charter, the most liberal that despot ever yet conferred."
>
> (1974:297–98)

The dialogue converts Rochester into a "three-tailed bashaw," explicitly connecting his Byronic imperiousness with the image of "Oriental despotism." This move is complicated by Jane's positioning within the scenario: stung by the "Eastern allusion" judging her "equivalent" to the "gazelle eyes" and "houri forms" of orientalist fantasy, Jane, with characteristic national pride, refers Rochester to the "bazaars of Stamboul" for such "slave purchases"; then threatens her own intervention "as a missionary," to produce a global charter of female emancipation that will curb her suitor's sexual despotism. The passage refers back and forward to the text's specific investment in English imperialism (through St. John's parallel missionary activity in India) and individualism (as the movement toward an inclusive feminism is circumvented by Jane's victory over her colonial rival, Bertha Mason).

I read this passage as exemplary of a significant intersection in nineteenth-century writing. Both Spivak (1985a) and Susan Meyer (1989) have recently discussed the role of imperial ideology in *Jane Eyre*. Spivak's landmark essay focuses on "the relationship between sexual reproduction and social subject-production—the dynamic nineteenth-century topos of feminism-in-imperialism" in *Jane Eyre*,

Frankenstein, and *Wide Sargasso Sea* (259), whereas Meyer deals with the figurative function of slavery, revolution, dark skin, and other characteristics of the colonized in *Jane Eyre*. This chapter is more concerned with examining the self-revealing logic with which a vocabulary and imagery of oppressed oriental womanhood are deployed in key nineteenth-century novels.[3]

The emergent modern woman, Jane must reject "the Eastern allusion" in the text of Western feminism she is inscribing with her life. At the same time, we will see that only this allusion makes possible the telling of Jane's story, supplying the vocabulary for the sexual risks faced by the unattached Englishwoman.[4] Brontë is not the first writer to cite "oriental misogyny" in her tale of Western women's oppression. The seraglio is a frequent reference point in Wollstonecraft's text, as it is in *Vanity Fair,* the novel I discuss in the second half of this chapter. In *The Newcomes,* Thackeray equates the mercenary marriage planned for his heroine, Ethel, with imaginary Brahmin women's lives through all the stages from forced marriage to sati. The novel's ultimate indictment of fashionable society is the parents' eagerness to offer their daughters to the polygamous Indian magnate, Rammun Loll. Jane Fairfax's bitter reference in *Emma* to "offices for the sale—not quite of human flesh—but of human intellect" (1985:300) demonstrates that Austen, as well as Brontë and Thackeray, could make the strategic allusion to the "bazaars of Stamboul." *Emma* also presents Jane's decision to seek employment as a governess in the language of ritual suicide: "With the fortitude of a devoted novitiate, she had resolved at one-and-twenty to complete the sacrifice, and retire from all the pleasures of life, of rational intercourse, equal society, peace and hope, to penance and mortification forever" (179).

In *Northanger Abbey,* a similar identification is made negatively through Henry Tilney's severe rejection of Catherine's lurid imaginings about his mother's incarceration and murder by her husband: "Remember that we are *English,* that we are *Christians.* . . . Does *our* education prepare us for such atrocities? Do *our* laws connive at them?" (1985:199; emphasis added). The irony of course is that Catherine's conjectures, though inaccurate in detail, are right in their perception of the General's brutal treatment of his wife and daughter.

In almost all these instances, the texts figure their heroines' lives through the very mechanisms of social and sexual control repeatedly produced in colonial discourse as incontrovertibly alien and repugnant practices of inferior cultures: polygamy, parda, and sati. But if these and similar identifications hint at an international sisterhood of suffering as the counterdiscourse of feminism engages with the processing of both "woman" and "orient" as subaltern categories, the slender consciousness of a wider female oppression seems to be always finally repressed or denied by the objectification of the colonized or imagined "oriental" female subject. The most familiar example is the text's deep ambivalence toward Bertha Mason, Rochester's supposedly mad Jamaican wife in *Jane Eyre,* an ambivalence reproduced in the contradictory critical responses to this figure.[5]

Bertha has received considerable attention as a manifestation of female repression and desire, a phenomenon documented in unprecedented detail by Gilbert and Gubar. But if the barely human prisoner caged in the Thornfield attic is the truest expression of women's anger and aspiration, these critics overlook that she is also the racial Other incarnate—a bestial, violent creature with an inordinate sexual appetite, caught in the colonized West Indies and confined "for her own good" by a master who has appropriated both her body and her wealth. Gilbert and Gubar identify the West Indian Creole, Bertha, as Jane Eyre's "truest and darkest double . . . the ferocious secret self Jane has been trying to repress" (1979:360). In their reading, Bertha—dark woman, dark double —functions as Jane's surrogate, acting out the incendiary desires Jane struggles to curb during her sufferings at Gateshead, Lowood, and Thornfield. But such a reading fails to register the cultural significance of the text's repression of Bertha. A ridge of burning heath, alive and devoured with flame, might be "a great emblem" (69) of Jane's feminist anger, while her friend Helen Burns might be named for the symbolic fires that eventually consume her in a fever of repressed rage, but neither the ardent Helen nor the fiery rebel, Jane, is the subject of the conflagration at the end of the novel.[6] In a carefully prepared displacement, the "Indian Messalina," Bertha, burns instead, succeeding at last in turning Thornfield into a pyre and killing herself at the same time (338).

This act of incineration provides the novel's consummation, at once securing Jane within the affiliations of monogamy, (colonial and local) property, and nuclear family, and freeing her into authorship. Spivak alludes to the cultural and historical inexorability of Bertha's consumption by the text when she writes: "[Bertha] must . . . act out . . . the transformation of her 'self' into that fictive Other, set fire to the house and kill herself, so that Jane Eyre can become the feminist individualist heroine of British fiction. I must read this as an allegory of the general epistemic violence of imperialism, the construction of a self-immolating colonial subject for the glorification of the social mission of the colonizer" (1985a:251).

If Jane Eyre is "the feminist individualist heroine of British fiction," Becky Sharp is her unacknowledged counterpart, working in submerged and serpentine ways toward similar social consolidations. This is not to suggest that the central impulse of Thackeray's canon is by any means feminist, but as inscribed in the text of Vanity Fair, the paired struggles of the orphan governess Becky and her inverse double, Amelia Sedley, parallel the feminist individualist aspirations embodied in Jane Eyre. "Becky's selfhood," Auerbach points out, "is less absolute than Jane's, but her powers are the same: she transforms every great house she enters, and by the end of the novel has become an inadvertent catalyst of social revolution" (1985:71). Like the notorious insurgent tendencies Lady Eastlake identified in Jane Eyre, Becky's revolutionary potential operates within circumscribed limits. She is finally responsible for the angelic Amelia's installation in domestic security. (Amelia's new husband Dobbin replaces the licentious George Osborne, resigns his Indian Commission, and begins writing a "History of the Punjaub"—a process paralleling Rochester's chastening as he gives up his colonial and continental adventuring to become, perforce, "a fixture" in England [1968:453]).

Like Jane Eyre, Thackeray's text records the consolidations of Victorianism. To cite Auerbach again: "By the end of the novel Becky has directly or indirectly killed off all the dominant Regency Bucks who obstructed the coming of the Victorian era" (72). So far unnoted among Becky's accomplishments is her agency in transforming her rakish husband Rawdon into a "deeply beloved" colonial governor in the Coventry islands, while permanently removing from the scene Jos Sedley, the exhausted and outdated Collector of Boggley Wollah (796). Similarly, the disreputable Sir Pitt Crawley is replaced by his decorous son, who takes "a strong part in the Negro Emancipation question" but sells his second seat in parliament to a supporter of slavery, a "Mr Quadroon with carte-blanche on the slave question" (121).

In both *Jane Eyre* and *Vanity Fair,* the mobility of the active female figure is connected with a certain dynamic of center and margins. This connection is apparent when the texts are dislocated from their insular English settings (the familiar worlds of Lowood, Thornfield, "the City," and so on). If the vocabulary of oriental misogyny operates in two ways, enabling the articulation of certain feminist concerns, but limiting their application within the constraints of the master discourse of empire, an examination of the historical and cultural construction of that vocabulary reveals (and unsettles) their cultural bases.[7] Joanna Liddle and Rama Joshi have shown how representing the oppression of Indian women, for example, was the ground of contestation between various groups— Indian and English, women and men. From about the early nineteenth century, women's oppression in India became an argument wielded both by those who maintained that Indians were unfit for self-rule and nationalist (men's and women's) groups who insisted that the colonial system sustained and often reinscribed women's oppression (1989:24–32).[8] The following pages read the cruxes of orientalism and feminism in these two contemporaneous novels, situating them within the newly visible imperial locations of the texts, as well as within a European discourse of oriental misogyny —particularly the charged cultural representations of polygamy and sati, produced in colonial discourse as uniform and constant practices of largely undifferentiated "oriental" cultures.[9]

ॐ

> *In a book published in England, it is observed, "there are some instances of remarkable generosity in the conduct of good wives, which would hardly gain credit with females differently educated. This, being interpreted, means, a good wife provides new wives for her husband."*
> —FANNY PARKS, WANDERINGS OF A PILGRIM
> IN SEARCH OF THE PICTURESQUE . . . WITH
> REVELATIONS OF LIFE IN THE ZENANA

When Mr. Brocklehurst denounces Jane as "worse than many a little heathen who says its prayers to Bhrama and kneels before Juggernaut," his missionary rhetoric is an early preparation for a conflict that preoccupies the second half of *Jane Eyre* and provides its final image (98). Spivak (1985a) has pointed out that Brontë's text of feminist self-realization does not end with a vision of Jane Rochester content in the seclusion of her achieved monogamy; rather, its last passages are devoted to her male obverse and counterpart, her restless cousin, St John Rivers, transfigured into "the warrior Greatheart" by his "labours for his race" in the imperial vineyard of India (477). St John's triumph at the end of the novel vindicates "the ambition of the high master spirit, which aims to fill a place in the first rank of those who are redeemed from the earth" (477), a beatification which cannot conceal the earthly and chauvinistic dimension of his achievement.

St John's activities refer back to a famous passage in *Jane Eyre,* the declaration Adrienne Rich has called "Brontë's feminist manifesto" (1979:97). Jane's assertion of her claim to the "field" of "effort" and excitement enjoyed by her brothers begins with an unsatisfactory survey of the inert English landscape: "I climbed the three staircases, raised the trapdoor of the attic and . . . looked out afar over sequestered hill, and along dim skyline . . . then I longed for a power which might overpass that limit; which might reach the busy world, regions full of life that I had heard of but never seen" (141). Jane's painful desire for action and excitement in her life as a governess is closely paralleled by St John's later account of his dissatisfaction with his country living, whose "uniform duties" weary him "to death": "I burned for the more active life of the world. . . . My life was so wretched, it must be changed, or I must die. After a season of darkness and struggling, light broke . . . my cramped existence all at once spread out to a plain without bounds. . . . The best qualifications of soldier, statesman and orator, were all needed: for all these centre in the good missionary. . . . I have vowed that I *will* overcome—and I leave Europe for the East." (388). The boundless plain of "the East" offers relief from the "sequestered" and inactive landscapes imprisoning both Jane and St John.

In St John's speech, as in the text's dynamics of money and power, empire is the active "field" of English exercise and effort: Jane's uncle leaves her the money he earned as a merchant in Madeira; Rochester derives his wealth from unnamed West Indian holdings; and most significantly, India is the field of St John's missionary exploits "for his race." It is the "field" Jane lays claim to in her manifesto and would choose as the ground of *her* efforts later on.[10] These scenes also have their parallel in *Villette,* where Lucy Snowe's passage to selfhood can be mapped outward from her survey of "the flat, rich middle of England" (104), to her heady viewing of the prospect from St Paul's, her outbound voyage against "the background . . . [of] a sky . . . grand with imperial promise, soft with tints of enchantment—[on which] strode from north to south a God-bent bow" (117), and finally her realization that "the spring which moved my energies lay far away beyond seas, in an Indian isle" (594). Like St John, Lucy establishes herself at the end as the agent of enlightenment and English rectitude among the superstitious corruptions of the "aboriginal" (145) Labassecour-iennes, "rondes, franches, brusques, et tant soit peu rebelles" (141).[11]

As in the other novels of the Chartist forties discussed earlier, empire functions in both Brontë and Thackeray as a space that complements and extends the unsatisfactory confines of England; in *Jane Eyre,* it is simultaneously the moral antithesis of home. In the scene vindicating Rochester's decision to leave Jamaica, character and integrity are summed up geographically, creating a subtext that will structure the pivotal choices of the plot as the antipodean alternatives of England or empire:

> "It was a fiery West Indian night; one of the description that frequently precede the hurricanes of those climates. . . . The air was like sulphur-streams. . . . Mosquitoes came buzzing in and hummed sullenly . . . the sea . . . rumbled dull like an earthquake . . . the moon was setting in the waves, broad and red, like a hot cannon ball. . . . And my ears were filled with the curses the maniac still shrieked out . . . no professed harlot ever had a fouler vocabulary than she."
>
> (335)

The horror of this alien scene explains Rochester's decision to deliver himself from the "bottomless pit" of Jamaica and "go home to God"(335)—in fact, a decision to incarcerate Bertha and embark on a bigamous search for "the antipodes of the Creole" (338). The immorality of this choice is disguised by a neat reversal which associates goodness with England, and blood, fire, and threatening sexuality with its geographical antithesis. The full vocabulary of savage otherness deployed here (hurricane, tempest, earthquake, mosquitoes, sulphur, fire, cannon) fuses with the more familiar Gothic element of *Jane Eyre,* as the environment of empire becomes the symbolic landscape of horror, and Bertha's uncontained rage and explicit sexuality the ultimate expression of un-Englishness.[12]

If empire proves a sulfurous hell for Rochester, its very fierceness provides a fit arena for St John, who deliberately "eschew[s] the calm of domestic life" for "the Himalayan ridge, or Caffre bush" (419). Jane, in contrast, is to be installed in "the calm of domestic life" with a forcibly settled Rochester ("he can't get out of England, I fancy, he's a fixture now," [453]); before attaining this English haven, however, she too is subject to the seductions of an oriental clime. This process of testing recalls Lucy Snowe's night of fevered temptation as she fights against the powerful "fascination" of that "hideous . . . Hindoo idol," Madame Walravens (558). In *Jane Eyre*, however, the sexual and social risks faced by the unattached woman are more systematically and persistently associated with a conflict of Eastern and Western alternatives, investing Jane's struggles with their deeper cultural resonance and complicating her connection with Bertha into one of confrontation rather than affiliation.

Jane's love for the early Rochester, the unregenerate despot of Thornfield, exposes her to two dangerous possibilities, both presented in the familiar language of oriental misogyny. The first, concealed in the romantic delusion of (feminine) self-abnegation, is easily detected in the sentimental verses Rochester sings to Jane:

> My love has placed her little hand
>   With noble faith in mine,
> And vowed that wedlock's sacred band
>   Our nature shall entwine.
>
> My love has sworn, with sealing kiss,
>   With me to live—to die.
> I have at last my nameless bliss:
>   As I love—loved am I!
>
> (301)

Rochester's song, packed with the inventory of Romanticism (rainbows, tides, ocean-surges), is deliberately calculated to reduce its object to swooning submission: "any other woman would have been melted to marrow at hearing such stanzas crooned in her praise" (301). Jane, however, must resist its invitation to self-annihilation; she "whets her tongue" as a "weapon of defence" and firmly denies any intention of self-sacrifice:

"What did he mean by such a pagan idea? *I* had no intention of
dying with him—he might depend on that."

"Oh, all he longed, all he prayed for, was that I might live with
him! Death was not for such as I."

"Indeed it was: I had as good a right to die when my time came
as he had: but I should bide that time, and not be hurried away in a
suttee."

(301)

Jane's "suttee" would be the logical consequence of "Wedlock's
sacred band" as here proposed by Rochester. Masquerading beneath his seductive persuasiveness is an overweening proprietorship requiring her own complete effacement. This masculine
possessiveness, characteristic of the lexicon sustaining nineteenth-
century Romanticism, is deliberately labeled "pagan." In both *Jane
Eyre* and *Vanity Fair*, as in Wollstonecraft's text, the Byronic tradition is highly suspect: Blanche Ingram affectedly "dote[s] on Cor-
sairs," and wants a modern Bothwell as a lover, while in *Vanity Fair*
Miss Crawley employs her enthusiasm for Fox and the French
Revolution to mask a lazy self-indulgence (208). Here, the text
translates Jane's refusal to be consumed by her lover's imperious
desire directly into the refusal to be "hurried away in a suttee": a
denial of his (inherently violent) fantasy of complete fusion, of an
ultimate consummation ignited by overwhelming female passion.

Jane must resist not only the seduction of her own annihilation
implicit in "wedlock's sacred band" but also its apparent opposite:
Rochester's "sultan"-like munificence, signifying a calculated will
to polygamy again designed to rob her of independent existence.
She is confronted once more by "the Eastern allusion" (338) when
Rochester discloses his deliberate search for a second bride, to
replace the "Indian Messalina" he is no longer "allured" by (333).
Rochester, in fact, acquires several possible substitutes for Bertha,
beginning with Adele's mother, the French Céline Varens, and
followed by "an Italian, Giacinta, and a German, Clara; both considered singularly handsome" (338). To this international collection, he also considers adding the lofty Blanche: "A strapper—a
real strapper, Jane: big, brown, and buxom; with hair just such as
the ladies of Carthage must have had" (248). Perceiving his unre-
lieved contempt for these women, whom he now compares to
slaves, Jane refuses to join Rochester's seraglio of exotics. Her
struggles against the "Eastern allusion," however, do not end with
her flight from Thornfield. St John Rivers' proposal exposes her

to the same temptation of female self-sacrifice she resisted in her relations with Rochester; this time, a seduction not of passion but of submission to St John, whose restless ambition so closely parallels her own.

Once compared to a worshiper of Brahma by Mr. Brocklehurst, and still yearning after her "broken idol" (379), Rochester, Jane is tempted to the service of yet another divinity. Whereas Lucy Snowe's love for the devoutly Catholic M. Paul might expose her to a grotesque theology of salvation in *Villette*—"Pour assurer vôtre salut là-haut, on ferait bien de vous brûler tout vive ici-bas" (148) —devotion to the profoundly Anglican creed of St John presents no lesser dangers in *Jane Eyre*. By marking her to complement his missionary labors in India, St John gains despotic power over Jane. His absolutism extends, "bashaw"-like, to a power of life and death.

St John's proposal is, in fact, a second invitation to self-immolation, as he makes clear when Jane rejects "martyrdom," by agreeing to go to India but refusing a loveless marriage: "Do you think God will be satisfied with half an oblation? Will He accept a mutilated sacrifice?" (430–31). But the burnt offering is for St John rather than his god. By going to India, Jane not only runs the risk of being "grilled alive in Calcutta," as her cousin Diana protests (441); married to St John, she will be scorched more surely and painfully by an internal flame: "But as his wife—at his side always, and always restrained, and always checked—forced to keep the fire of my nature continually low, to compel it to burn inwardly and never utter a cry, though the imprisoned flame consumed vital after vital—*this* would be unendurable" (433). To marry St John, in fact, would be another means for Jane to "be hurried away in a suttee," the inner glow and blaze of her passionate nature consuming her as surely as any external flame.

So far I have indicated in deliberate detail the extent of the submerged vocabulary of oriental misogyny within the familiar narrative of *Jane Eyre*. To reveal the cultural significance of this language, the text's repeated application of the allusions of polygamy and sati to the sexual and moral temptations of the unfriended woman must be mapped simultaneously against another scheme: on a fault line of moral differentiation between empire and England, romantic thralldom and growing feminist consciousness, false worship and missionary exaltation. To chart the correspondence between these separate registers, the novel's deployment of "oriental misogyny"—and especially of sati—must be located within its construction in two key discourses of the period.

Sati was a natural figure for feminist polemic in Victorian England, as Dorothy K. Stein elaborates:

> Suttee did not occur in England, but many manifestations of the attitudes and anxieties underlying the practice did. Nineteenth-century respectability in both Britain and India divided women into exalted and degraded classes, not only on the basis of actual or imputed sexual behavior, but also on the basis of whether that behavior was at all times controlled and supervised, preferably by a male connection. . . . Both societies agreed to disadvantage those women who could not obtain suitable male protection. These were not simply shared general attitudes. They found expression in numerous specific parallels. . . . Most revealing of all, however, was the discussion that arose out of the recognition that England too possessed a sizable group of unmarriageable, and hence anomalous, women of good breeding.
>
> (1978:266)[13]

In *Vanity Fair,* Becky manages, by sacrificing her sexual respectability, to turn her unattached status murderously back upon the society that excludes her; Jane's vulnerability to the "oriental" temptations of self-annihilation represented by Rochester and St John, on the other hand, stems naturally from her situation as an unattached woman who is "quite a lady" (123).

Both Brontë and Thackeray clearly recognize the threat of the growing class of "unnecessary" women and the force religion and convention brought to containing them. Lowood is an institution dedicated to the strict management, if not the calculated eradication, of this potentially destabilizing class. Helen Burns' submission to a doctrine of chastisement and Eliza Reed's immurement in a convent suggest other forms of women's control through organized religion. Perhaps even more telling in its linking of systems for domestic and imperial control is Brontë's scathing commentary in *Shirley* on the activity and excitement provided to unoccupied women in English villages by "the Jew basket" and the "Missionary basket," means of fund raising for the conversion of non-Christians throughout the empire, a means of emotional regulation recalling the spinster Lady Emily's absorbing and absurd missionary "correspondences with clerical gentlemen throughout our East and West India possessions" in *Vanity Fair* (392).

This context of religious control illuminates James Mill's 1817 assertion that "of the modes adopted by Hindus of sacrificing themselves to divine powers, none . . . has more excited the attention of Europeans than the burning of wives upon the funeral piles of their husbands" (quoted, Sharma 1976:598). Sati had generated intense popular and literary interest in Europe since the previous century; in England, it featured luridly in early Romantic texts, such as Southey's best-selling *The Curse of Kehama* (1817), as well as in several forgotten "oriental tales."[14] Conant's 1908 study, *The Oriental Tale in England in the Eighteenth Century*, lists dozens of references to sati. Although adapted during the eighteenth century by several prominent writers in Britain, and an evident force in the early Romanticism of Southey, Byron, and Scott, the "Oriental Tale" was primarily a French genre. Dorothy Figueira points out that French writers of diverse leanings appropriated sati to a range of private concerns: Voltaire employed it to attack both priestly control (in *Questions sur l'Encyclopédie*) and female constancy (in *Zadig*); the traveler Pierre Sonnerat (cited by Southey) initiated a persistent European tradition of eroticization, in which sati marked a "fallen" woman's redemption as she proved an undiminished femininity by following her lover's corpse into the flames (Figueira 1988:5–6).

Having become a widely accessible European symbol, sati could function simultaneously as an emblem of female oppression through which Western women represented their own struggles. This emblematic use of sati is poignantly exemplified in Figueira's anecdote of the German Romantic poet Karoline von Gunderrode. Gunderrode killed herself on the banks of the Rhine, leaving as a suicide note a Sanskrit poem about sati. Figueira comments: "What precisely brought Gunderrode to her death is less consequential than the fact that, with this poem, she sought to ennoble her own despair. . . . On a larger scale Gunderrode's poetic testimony and her death are emblematic of the forces involved in exoticism and exemplify the fruits born of the literary meeting between East and West" (3).[15]

As Figueira's comment suggests, sati, produced in Western discourse, was an ambiguous emblem at best, speaking at once of an enhanced and romanticized universal female suffering and the manufacture of an alien and exotic "Orient." In the middle decades of the nineteenth century, this second meaning was reinforced by political expediency as "the Indo-Western encounter became largely an Indo-British encounter" (Sharma 1976:592):

"Whereas earlier the abolition of Suttee had been a joint humanist enterprise in which the Government, the missionaries, and enlightened native opinion had come together on a common platform, from now on, the case of Suttee was to be argued in terms of imperialism. Suttee, on account of its dramatic nature, became an element in the vindication of British Imperialism . . . [and] was also used as a moral justification to the Britishers to impose their rule on India" (Sharma 1976:601–2).

The issue of sati acquired unprecedented urgency in the decades leading up to the uprising of 1857. Bengal, the premier British holding in India, registered an outbreak of female immolation early in the century.[16] Lata Mani suggests that English attempts to manage or regulate sati by distinguishing between "illegal" and "legal" burnings only served to increase its visibility, nearly tripling its incidence in three years.[17] As one colonial policeman commented dryly, "authorising a practice is not the way to effect its gradual abolition" (quoted, Mani 1985:111). The act was finally criminalized in 1829, but as Spivak has pointed out, this criminalization was a significant marking of how sati had been read in Western discourse. Among available classifications for the act of sati were religious martyrdom and warlike heroism, "with the husband standing in for sovereign or State, for whose sake an intoxicating ideology of sacrifice can be mobilized. In the event, it was categorized with murder, infanticide and the lethal exposure of the very old. The dubious place of the free will of the constituted sexed subject as female was successfully effaced" (Spivak 1985b:125).[18]

Criminalization also enhanced the potency of sati as a cultural symbol in England. Sharma traces two related features of the English response: "It became necessary for British writers to *sensationalize* Suttee on the one hand, and for British historians to *monopolize* the credit for having abolished it on the other" (1976:604). Throughout the mid–nineteenth century, sati continued to provide justification both for empire and for increased missionary penetration. Meanwhile, English art indulged in picturesque arrangements of the moment of immolation. Paul B. Courtright characterizes the nineteenth century as the era of "the picturesque sati." James Atkinson's famous painting of a supplicant and barebreasted sati looking to heaven (and England) for deliverance was exhibited as late as 1841.[19] These linked messages of sensationalization and monopolization are present in the subtext of *Jane Eyre*

—in the rhetoric of St John's missionary fervor and in Jane's repeated denunciations of oriental misogyny—as well as in writings such as Thackeray's "Problematic Invasion of British India" (1844), an essay justifying Company rule on the grounds of its abolition of evils like sati, thuggee, and infanticide.[20]

Brontë's novel, located where the discourse of women's oppression intersects with an increasingly violent imperialist discourse of oriental misogyny, derives its most powerful image from this convergence. Sati had become a figure loaded with divergent political messages: of Western feminism, of English imperialism and racism, and of European Romanticism. "I really don't think that English women are given to flaming, and burning, and melting, and being generally combustible on ordinary occasions, as we are led by one or two novelists to suppose," Rhoda Broughton's heroine claims in the 1899 novel *Cometh Up as a Flower*, defending her countrywomen from the charge of excessive sexuality, an accusation frequently made against the novels of Broughton herself and against her fellow novelists Mary Braddon and Ellen (Mrs. Henry) Wood. But, as Elaine Showalter recognizes, "escape from sexual bonds and family networks rather than sexual frustration or gratification" was the impulse behind these fictions of female "flamings and burnings" (1978:105).[21]

The association of both sexual yearning and feminist rage with the literal and figurative flames of passion feeds directly into the central image of *Jane Eyre*. Since Dido's fiery death in the *Aeneid*, European literary tradition had associated female immolation with love: a burning passion which could be exhausted only in death, a connection reinforced over the last century by the eroticization of sati. Although the cultural rhetoric of empire produced such an act as incontrovertibly other and foreign, feminist consciousness suggested that sati spoke also of a wider female oppression, while at the same time effacing the subjecthood of its voiceless oriental "objects." All these meanings coalesce in the ultimate sati of *Jane Eyre*, the death of the caged madwoman, Bertha, whose unmanageable sexuality is the most threatening sign of both racial and female otherness. The rooftop at Thornfield, site of Jane's "manifesto" of feminist individualism, becomes by a fitting logic the flaming backdrop for Bertha's inarticulate shouts as the caged woman gestures defiantly over the sequestered English landscape, then ambiguously meets her death as Rochester approaches to "save" her.

ॐ

Western *representations of the harem are . . . the
fulfillment of the wish to uncover what is hidden. If
the depicted is orientalised, the depicting activity is
obviously Western. . . .*

The harem can thus be considered as a mise-
en-scène, *displaced onto the Orient, of the meta-
physics of man and woman: a machinery producing
an ontology of the Western concept of man and
woman. . . .*

*The order of the harem is organised around the
limitless pleasure of the Master, above all his sexual
pleasure which starts with his scopic privilege. . . .
The harem is a solitary confinement for all and is
a delicious place for one person only—the Master.*

*The Master's primal object of enjoyment and
possession is not so much woman as women. With
polygamy, he does not possess the other sex, but its
multiplicity. Multiplicity characterises inferiority . . .
the amount of women will never match the uniqueness
of the Master.*

　　　—*Olivier Richon*, "REPRESENTATION, THE
　　　　　　　　　　DESPOT AND THE HAREM"

Sexual despotism, figured in the harem and its Master, is the
most direct intertextual link between *Jane Eyre* and *Vanity Fair*. In
the highly suggestive charade scenes, part of the multiple enact-
ments of counterfeit marriages at the center of *Jane Eyre*, Rochester weds Blanche Ingram "in the pantomime of a marriage," then,
"the very model of an Eastern Emir," plays the surrogate suitor
espousing Rebecca with golden bracelets at the well (212–13). The
sequence ends, prophetically, with Rochester fettered in *Bride*well
prison and is followed by the more sinister charade of his at-
tempted bigamy with Jane. The narration of Rochester's "false"
entry into wedlock with Bertha and of his unsuccessful liaisons
with Céline, Clara, and Giacinta forms the last of these representations. In each, Rochester's role remains the same: metropolitan
Englishman in Jamaica, eligible county landowner, or rich employer, he is always the Master; the bride figure in these sham
marriages appears, by contrast, infinitely variable. Jane's passage

to success is the process of her cultural and moral differentiation from this pool of interchangeable unfit wives.

The harem is a familiar scene of English literature from Purchas' 1610 collection of travel narratives to James Morrier's 1824 *The Adventures of Hajji Baba, of Ispahan.* Throughout *Vanity Fair,* the oriental harem is employed to comment on English sexual practices, in addition to operating as a key reference in the charade sequence so reminiscent of *Jane Eyre.*[22] The sinister Lord Steyne deals with insubordination in his "Hareem" no more despotically than George Osborne does with Amelia (567). "We are Turks with the affections of our women," the narrator cries despairingly of Amelia's secret sufferings: "We let their bodies go about liberally enough with smiles and ringlets . . . instead of veils and yakmaks. But their souls must be seen by only one man, and they obey not unwillingly" (216). The focus here shifts from the multiplicity of the harem to its imposed seclusion. This is a characteristic concern; in colonial discourse, the veil and other practices of female seclusion and parda (different in origin, history, and practice) were received primarily as signs of obstruction and concealment in the all-conquering gaze of the European spectator.[23]

Frantz Fanon has described the menace presented in the spectacle of the veiled Algerian woman through the different stages of (de)colonization: first as an instance of resistance to the colonizer's *knowing;* and later as a probable representative of the Resistance, weapons concealed beneath her veil (1967b).[24] In earlier accounts, the secluded "oriental" woman, read as a sign of the colonizer's exclusion, was more often the *site* of confrontation and contest than a victim to be rescued from "oriental misogyny"—much less the subject of her own experience. In E. M. Forster's liberal imagination, a symbolic violation of parda marks the homoerotic reconciliation between colonizing and colonized men as Aziz *shows* Fielding his wife's photograph in *A Passage to India*—a moment of Forsterian connection, transacted through the objectified image of a woman who is unnamed, voiceless, and dead.

In nineteenth-century Romanticism, the harem was an object of voyeuristic scrutiny and speculation, even as it was widely deplored as the source of the oriental oppression of women. Titles like Fanny Parks' *Wanderings of a Pilgrim Search of the Picturesque . . . with Revelations of Life in the Zenana* (1850) suggest the nature of contemporary interest. As Kiernan points out, both Byron's Don

Juan and Scott's character in *Peveril of the Peak* (1823) manage to
penetrate the harem, while Goldsmith, Johnson, and Boswell fan-
tasize such acts in their private writings (1986:135–38).[25] In his
Notes on a Journey from Cornhill to Grand Cairo, the account of a tour
sponsored by the Peninsular and Oriental Company in 1844,
Thackeray himself admits to a "strange feeling of curiosity" in "ill
regulated minds" as his gaze probes the grated palace windows of
Istanbul, longing "just to have *one* peep, one look at all those
wondrous beauties . . . [and] gaudy black slaves" (1869:413).
Thackeray's imagination is also deliciously tickled by the fancy that
the smooth Bosphorus over which he is sailing might conceal the
body of some "luckless beauty" murdered by her jealous possessor:
"They say it is death to pick up any of the sacks thereabouts, if a
stray one should float by you. There were none any day I passed,
at least, on the surface of the water" (413; original emphasis).[26] A
similar blend of horror and fascination motivates the narrator to
peer uncomfortably, one hand checking his beard for reassurance,
into the women's quarters of Vanity Fair, at "the poor secret
martyrs and victims . . . stretched out on racks in bedrooms
and . . . into those dark places where torture is administered"
(662).

Western indignation over the seraglio, like the sensationalized
rhetoric denouncing sati, is historically and culturally problematic,
carrying its own impulses of violation and trespass. The charade
sequence in *Vanity Fair* is characterized by these same ambiguities,
as voyeurism and the tensions of imperial and racial domination
complicate its message of female oppression, while the introduction of an *Eothen*-like "oriental traveler" brings the element of
Exoticism directly into play. The first and most detailed charade,
set in a carefully orientalized location, is staged by the explorer,
Bedwin Sands, who uses his real-life black servant and other Eastern acquisitions to lend authenticity to his production. The first
act presents an unsuccessful attempt by "a Turkish voluptuary" to
purchase a Circassian woman from a Nubian slave dealer. As the
scene opens:

> Mesrour the Nubian appears, with bare arms, bangles, yata-
> ghans, and every Eastern ornament—gaunt, tall, and hideous. . . .
> He makes a salaam before my lord the Aga.
> A thrill of terror and delight runs through the assembly. The
> ladies whisper to one another. The black slave was given to Bedwin

Sands by an Egyptian Pasha in exchange for three dozen of maraschino. He has sewn up ever so many odalisques in sacks and tilted
them into the Nile.

(594)

This opening scene, Maria DiBattista writes in a 1980 essay on
the Clytemnestra figure in *Vanity Fair,* recalls a moment when the
lordly George Osborne thrills to receive Amelia's adoration: "He
saw a slave before him in that simple yielding faithful creature,
and his soul within him thrilled secretly somehow. . . . He would
be generous-minded, Sultan as he was, and raise up this kneeling
Esther and make a queen of her" (237–38). DiBattista's essay is a
compelling account of the "sexual despotism" operative in both
scenes. When she links the audience's thrill at the sight of the
enslaved Nubian with their complicity in George's thrill of power
and possession as he gazes at the abject Amelia, however, her
emphasis seems to elide the particular historical and cultural significance of the all-male Aga/Slave-Dealer/Slave configuration in
this Victorian production.

Absent from the charade, but behind the scenes, is Mesrour's
actual master, Bedwin Sands, who, in the framing production of
the explorer's tale has successfully bartered his servant for "three
dozen maraschino." DiBattista declares: "Despite the exotic decor
evoking an alien, barbaric milieu, the initial moments of this charade announce *a universal, not a historically localized, cultural pathol-
ogy:* sexual bondage, enslavement, exploitation and victimization"
(1980:829; emphasis added). Not apprehended in the anxiety to
highlight what the essay calls "the icons of sexual imperialism" in
the scene is that the orientalist language in which the passage
abounds is not a transparent *metaphor* of sexual oppression but is
itself a powerful image of domination, with a very specific "historically localized" application. The secret sensation of pleasurable
excitement aroused in these spectators by the salaams of the deco-
rated Nubian is, first of all, a *racial* thrill—the recreation of the
scene of "oriental" barter, an act of scopic mastery.

In DiBattista's essay, the figure of the male Nubian is conflated
with the Circassian female slave and read primarily as a coded
message of *sexual* domination, a reading which allows little interpretive space for the racial difference manifested in the Nubian's most significant attribute: blackness. The form of the adorned,
bare-armed, and "hideous" Nubian, I want to suggest, refers back

to a second dark figure occluded in most readings of *Vanity Fair:* the "Black princess" (245), Rhoda Swartz, whose story, incorporating both racial and sexual difference, forms a shadowy and repressed commentary on the sexual careers of Becky and Amelia. A Mulatto heiress from St. Kitts who "pays double" at Miss Pinkerton's Academy, Miss Swartz appears first as an "impetuous and woolly-headed, but generous and affectionate" (43) fellow boarder, hysterical with grief at parting from Amelia. If Rhoda's excessive sensibility is somewhat ridiculous, it makes her immediately akin to the novel's other ridiculously affectionate and unjudging creature, Amelia; at the same time, her obscure and suspect history (she is the daughter of a "German Jew—a slave owner, they say— connected with the Cannibal Islands" [245]) links her to the murderous siren, Becky.

As a colonial heiress with "I don't know how many plantations in the West Indies . . . and three stars to her name, in the East India stockholders' list" (244), Miss Swartz is courted by both Mayfair and City society; among her pursuers is George's father, the "honest British merchant" whose House represents the unsavory Swartz interests in the metropolis. Like Amelia, Miss Swartz is enraptured by George: if George is Amelia's "Europe: her emperor: her allied monarchs and august prince regent" (151), Miss Swartz is his other ready slave, "adorn[ing] herself . . . to meet her conqueror" (251). The submissiveness of both Amelia and Rhoda before George enacts the Nubian slave's prostration before the Aga, but where the narrator shows a rueful sympathy for Amelia's sexual vulnerability, Rhoda receives more ambiguous treatment as George conciliates and flirts with this "perfect Belle Sauvage," (244) though he declines to marry her.

With an allusiveness characteristic of *Vanity Fair*, George's sexual contempt for Rhoda is revealed only in glancing references: "Osborne is a devil of a fellow," a fellow soldier confides: "There was a judge's daughter at Demarara went almost mad about him; then there was that beautiful quadroon girl . . . at St Vincent's, you know" (155). The nature of George's sexual adventures in the West Indies is annotated by the phrase he uses about Rhoda, describing her angrily to his father as the "Hottentot Venus" (256), a reference whose shocking connotations of unnatural and bestial sexuality are mostly lost in modern readings.

"The Hottentot Venus" was a title originally applied to Saartjie Baartman, a twenty-year-old Khoi-khoin woman exhibited in London and Paris from 1810 to 1815, and later to a second African woman displayed at a ball by the Duchess Du Barry in 1829. Sander Gilman shows that widely familiar illustrations and caricatures represented the "Hottentot Venus" in profile or rear view with exaggeratedly large buttocks (and, after her death and dissection by Cuvier, with supposedly "aberrant" genitalia, referred to as "the Hottentot Apron").[27] George's reference to the "Hottentot Venus" must, then, be read as a brutal allusion to the sexuality of the colonized woman, a sexuality he exploits during his West Indian campaign but (like Rochester) rejects wholesale in a wife.

In his analysis of icons of female sexuality, Gilman has argued that nineteenth-century art associates "the central [white] female figure . . . with a black female in such a way as to imply their sexual similarity" (1985:209). The inscription of racial difference, however, always makes that identification problematic: if Rhoda and George's other West Indian conquests suggest the multiplicity and variety of his sexual slaves, they are also simultaneously discounted as true subjects of that experience. The grotesque representation of Rhoda Swartz, no less than the Gothic horror concentrated in Bertha Mason, marks the intersection of sexual and racial difference. Both women are simultaneously defined through an inheritance of unnatural size, genetic contamination (madness, cannibalism), and gargantuan sexual appetite—attributes of racial difference that exclude them from true kinship with white female subjects even as they share a similar sexual subjection.

Both Bertha Mason and Rhoda Swartz are offspring of interracial unions, a characteristic that has especially sinister connotations throughout the Thackeray canon (Davies 1961:326–31). Rhoda's story connects not only with those of her literary counterparts, the exiled parlor-boarders in two unfinished texts, Austen's *Sanditon* and Brontë's *Emma,* but to a third child of miscegenation, the "poor Mrs Blechyndon" of Thackeray's autobiographical writings.[28] This illegitimate half sister, the product of his father's early life in India, recurs in Thackeray's diaries and letters as a source of somewhat facile guilt and self-chastisement: "Went to Bedford and dined on turtle and cold beef—I wish the turtle had choked me—there is poor Mrs Blechyndon starving in India, whilst I am gorging in this unconscionable way here" (1964,1:245). Whereas in Thackeray's letters his "black" sister is directly deprived of her metropolitan inheritance (1964,2:32), in *Vanity Fair* Rhoda, described in a telling reversal of terms as "the dark object of [a] conspiracy" (250) to possess her wealth, marries the aristocratic James M'Mull as a result of her guardian's machinations. Both shadowy, unrealized figures, Mrs. Blechyndon—her name never appears in the correspondence—and Miss Swartz—or "Swartz," as she is often referred to in the text—mark the uneasy return of the effaced, disinherited colonial woman in Thackeray's public as well as private narratives.

A famous passage in *Vanity Fair* describes the siren's tail and is often read as an allusion to female sexuality; it could be applied as easily to the submerged and invisible operations of Thackeray's text: "Those who like may peep down under waves that are pretty transparent and see it writhing and twirling . . . flapping amongst bones, or curling round corpses; but above the waterline, I ask, has not everything been proper, agreeable and decorous?. . . We had best not examine the fiendish marine cannibals, revelling and feasting" (738). The surface of *Vanity Fair* remains calm and smooth, like the river Bosphorus in the *Cape to Cairo* narrative, *"at least, on the surface of the water,"* but beneath—half-seen, half-sensed—are female bodies in sacks as well as "fiendish marine cannibals." While Rhoda Swartz, "the Black Princess," of *Vanity Fair* is explicitly "connected with the Cannibal Islands," the actions of "fiendish marine cannibals" require underwater detective techniques.

Musselwhite's intriguing reading of *Vanity Fair* alongside Marx's *Eighteenth Brumaire of Louis Bonaparte* claims that both texts enact in their variety of styles and forms the breakdown of representation that was the chief feature of the revolutionary year 1848 (1987:123–40). Whereas in *Jane Eyre* the insurrectionary aspirations of Chartism at home and revolution in Europe are absorbed and almost contained within the form of a feminist autobiography of individual "hunger, rebellion and rage," Thackeray's narrative response to the same crises is at once more fragmented and more wide ranging. Its interest, "those mutations which age produces in empires, cities and boroughs" mapped through the (domestic and martial) histories of paired female protagonists (101).

Nowhere is the complicated pattern of historical and formal "mutations" in *Vanity Fair* enacted more clearly than in the charade sequence. Where the first scene ends with the possibility of revolt and assassination as the servant Mesrour turns on the Aga, the second transforms the potential of mutiny in the orient to a scene of pacification: to the incongruous European medley of Mozart's

Magic Flute, a "comic song . . . by Mr Wagg," and a transplanted
version of an appropriated battle tune, "The Camels are Coming,"
the Circassian slave, Zuleikah, is shown "perfectly reconciled" to
her purchaser, while "the Kislar Aga has become a peaceful black
slave" (595). Although the images of sexual subjection and menace
continue in the following charades with Becky prophetically figured as Clytemnestra, the troubling images of colonial unrest are
successfully contained by the transforming cultural presence of
Europe. In the final sequence again, a stormy ocean scene, performed to the music of "Rule Britannia," is replaced by the calm-
ing sounds of Becky's nightingale voice.[29]

At the same time, however, the mutations and revolutions of
"empires, cities and boroughs" are also enacted within Thackeray's
metropolis. If *Jane Eyre* outlines a landscape of "antipodean" moral
alternatives between England and empire, Thackeray's map of
England is more minutely constituted: "Minto Square, Great Clive
Street, Warren Street, Hastings Street, Ochterlony Place, Plassy
Square, Assaye Terrace . . . who does not know these respectable
abodes of the retired Indian aristocracy, and the quarter which Mr
Wenham calls the Black Hole, in a word?" (693–94). Inscribed in
the topography of London, this imperial history recalls not only
the triumphs of the glorious past but, equally, imperial defeats:
the failed Napoleonic ambitions of the novel's present, as well as
the competing imperial aspirations of 1848. The historical stage of
Vanity Fair encompasses Plassey as well as Waterloo, Clive, and the
old campaigner Wellington—like Dobbin, a former India hand:
"But where was it he learned his art?" (334)—as well as various
Bonapartes. All these alike evoke the name of "famous actions":
their "tale is in every Englishman's mouth"(385).

If the fantasized oriental scene of the charades is easily pacified
by musical representations of Europe, the physical scene of London is less easily altered. In *Vanity Fair,* unlike in *Jane Eyre,* disturbing colonial presences are neither consumed nor easily expelled.
If the "Eastern allusion" is amputated from Jane Rochester's autobiography by Bertha's removal, St John's exile, and Rochester's
reformation, the more deeply historical narrative of *Vanity Fair*
instead absorbs and internalizes that allusion. At the end of the
first section of the novel, Rhoda and her wealth are silently assimi-
lated into the impeccable English society of Hampton Court, to
reappear in the last chapters as Amelia returns, secure in her
comfortable—if not companionate—marriage to the retired sol-

dier Dobbin. The two settle down to respectable domesticity in London's Anglo-Indian quarter, or "Black Hole," a name recalling simultaneously the dark places of sexual torture, the murky depths of the Bosphorus, *and* the authorizing and controlling mythology of imperial history, even as the fissures of the women's lives are covered by a triumphant Victorianism.

five

"All the Girls Say Serve Him Right": The Multiple Anxieties of Edwin Drood

> *Suez is the Centre of our life work. We shall carry out the act for which the world is waiting to proclaim that we are male!*
> — **PROSPER ENFANTIN**[1]
>
> *Sing Yeh, my cruel John Chinaman,*
> *Sing Yeo, my stubborn John Chinaman*
> *Not Cobden himself can take off the ban*
> *By humanity laid on John Chinaman.*
> . . . .
> *Sing lie-tea, my sly Chinaman*
> *No fightee, my coward John Chinaman,*
> *John Bull has a chance—let him, if he can*
> *Somewhat open the eyes of John Chinaman.*
> — **PUNCH**, *1858*
>
> *I shall then go engineering into the East, and Pussy with me.*
> — **EDWIN DROOD**

*C*HINA AND Egypt; European male prowess and the boring of canals through conquered land; John Bull and his antitypes, the radical Cobden and that Other John, John Chinaman: *The Mystery of Edwin Drood* orchestrates these central concerns of empire, but my reading of its convergent motifs begins with the domestic, with something as localized, in fact, as an unhappy engagement. Edwin Drood and Rosa Bud walk through Cloisterham, reluctant lovers, to "the Lumps-of-Delight shop." Rosa has just refused to kiss

Edwin because she has "an acidulated drop" in her mouth (1986:55). The only way she can bear their intimacy is to pretend she and Edwin will not have to be married one day soon; for this reason she restrains her annoyance at his "rather indignant" rejection of her Turkish Delights: "Call yourself an Engineer and not know *that?*" (58) To avoid a quarrel, the two begin to invent a perfect love for Edwin, a woman unlike Rosa in every respect:

> "And this most sensible of creatures likes the idea of being carried off to Egypt; does she, Eddy?"
> "Yes. She takes a sensible interest in the triumphs of engineering skill: especially when they are to change the whole condition of an undeveloped country."
> "Lor!" says Rosa. . . . "Doesn't she hate boilers and things?"
> "I can answer for her not being so idiotic as to hate Boilers," he returns. . . .
> "But don't she hate Arabs, and Turks, and Fellahs, and people?"
> "Certainly not." Very firmly.
> "At least she *must* hate the Pyramids? . . . Ah! you should hear Miss Twinkleton," often nodding her head, and much enjoying the Lumps, "bore about them. . . . Tiresome old burying-grounds!. . . And then there was Belzoni or somebody, dragged out by the legs, half-choked. . . . All the girls say serve him right, and hope it hurt him, and wish he had been quite choked."[2]
> The two youthful figures, side by side, but not now arm-in-arm, wander discontentedly about the Old Close. . . .
> "Well," says Edwin, after a lengthy silence. "According to custom. We can't get on, Rosa."
> Rosa tosses her head, and says she don't want to get on.
>
> (59–60)

The tension between the couple—a tension fueled by their mutual reluctance to fulfill a marriage contract, by Edwin's casual contempt for Rosa, by Rosa's entrapment in an engagement decreed by paternal whim and reinforced through the institutional pressures of Miss Twinkleton's academy—focuses in this scene on an argument about empire. Rosa "hates" it all equally: "Arabs, and Turks and Fellahs, and people" as well as orientalist archaeologists and engineers. The archaeologists and engineers, "boring" in their different and similar ways—in their penetration of colonized earth or of colonized history, and in how their admirers "bore about them"—are the producers of the former, constructing "Arabs . . . and Fellahs and people" simultaneously with "pyramids" and boilers and canals, all equally the paraphernalia of imperial conquest and progress.

Edwin, boring in these senses, also embodies a particular sexual thrust; his will to "change the whole condition of an undeveloped country" is the counterpart of the proprietary assurance he displays with Rosa. Edwin's ordained rights over Rosa are an established principle of society: "The Nun's House is never in such a state of flutter as when this allotted husband calls to see little Rosebud. (It is unanimously understood by the young ladies that he is lawfully entitled to this privilege, and that if Miss Twinkleton disputed it she would be instantly taken up and transported)" (54). Edwin's assumed (pre)conjugal rights are, in fact, *territorial* rights; they confer, among other things, an extended license to infantilize and debase. This license emerges, predictably, in a range of interactions with "inferiors" of every sort, as in the lordly demand that Mrs. Tope "give me a kiss, because its Pussy's birthday": "I'd Pussy you, young man, if I was Pussy, as you call her," Mrs. Tope retorts. "Your uncle's too much wrapt up in you. . . . He makes so much of you that its my opinion you think you've only to call your Pussys by the dozen, to make 'em come" (45).

The forcibly "saluted" landlady is not the only one to resent Edwin's "pet name" for Rosa. A far more telling reproof administered by her guardian, Mr. Grewgious, finally chastens Edwin but not before he has infuriated Neville Landless with the same arrogant presumption of ownership. Another displaced child of the imperial system reared outside the metropolitan confines of England, Neville's deprivation is inscribed in his name: he lacks Edwin's natural title to the territorial certitudes of empire. Neville's resentment of Edwin's complacency and his instinctive championship of the absent Rosa culminate in a scene that curiously recalls the previous exchange between Edwin and Rosa. Edwin's condescending announcement that he is "going to wake up Egypt a little" (96) leads to a patronizing comparison of his own busy life of "doing, working, engineering" (97) with Neville's scholarship. Neville is feminized into irrelevance by this perceived inactivity ("you readers, who ought to know everything" [98]), just as Rosa was earlier dismissed and infantilized as "idiotic," "a little . . . Goose," and, of course, "Pussy" (59).

Nor is this the end of the scene between the two men: Neville is not only sexually suspect because of his inaptitude for "doing, working, engineering," but also racially compromised. In his notes for *Edwin Drood,* Dickens gave Neville and his sister, Helena, an "imperceptibly acquired mixture" of "Oriental blood." The novel puts the connection more ambiguously in Neville's confidences about their childhood in Ceylon: "I have been brought up among abject and servile dependents, of an inferior race, and I may easily have contracted some affinity with them. Sometimes, I don't know but that it may be a drop of what is tigerish in their blood" (90).[3]

The Landlesses' "tigerish" affinities may be innate or acquired, but they serve to tint the brother and sister with an oriental otherness. The Landlesses' aura of difference, their un-English air of being hunted rather than pursuers, provokes Edwin's hostility toward Neville; the same sensation is expressed toward Neville's female counterpart, Helena, as an instant sexual attraction. This unspoken attraction is the other source of antagonism between the two men, adding a further dimension to the sexual and imperial aggression already displayed in Edwin's exchange with Rosa. If Helena's disturbing exotic challenge can be absorbed within a scheme of heterosexual desire already based on domination and subjection, Neville presents a different problem.[4] To Edwin at least, Neville is an intruder and alien in Cloisterham: the land Neville comes from is "a long way off, I believe? . . . That part of the world is at a safe distance" (102). Landless, Neville becomes representative of other dispossessed (and so naturally inferior) peoples. The quarrel between the two, beginning as an argument about Edwin's "proprietorship" of Rosa, turns inevitably into a racial encounter with Neville: "You may know a black common fellow . . . when you see him (and no doubt you have a large acquaintance that way); but you are no judge of white men" (102). The development of the scene reveals Edwin's racial and sexual arrogance as almost indistinguishable, the two meshing inextricably with his urge to imperial domination.

"This insulting allusion to his dark skin," the passage continues, "infuriates Neville to . . . [a] violent degree" (90). (He is, after all, the self-hating hybrid, soon to become a tiresomely familiar type in fiction.) All that is needed to make Neville the prime suspect in Edwin's murder is for the novel's other unnaturally dark man, Edwin's loving uncle Jasper, to ferment the quarrel between the two young men. Jasper, the choirmaster of Cloisterham, is, like Neville, excluded from the active classes of empire; as an artist and musician, he too resents Edwin's arrogant sense of mastery and mission ("I shall then go engineering into the East, and Pussy with me" [50]). Mrs. Tope's goaded rejoinder to Edwin's kiss has already linked his offensive sexual assurance with Jasper's extreme devotion to his nephew, a devotion Edwin himself describes as "almost womanish" (168). Jasper's public display of affection for Edwin masks a complex blend of contempt, envy, and passion, a mix that also encompasses the tension between the distinct groups of winners and losers brought into being by empire.

In *Between Men* Sedgwick discusses the racially charged homo-erotic triangles of *Edwin Drood:* the tragic threesome Jasper, Edwin, and Neville is highlighted against the more benign relationship of Neville to his solidly English mentor, the minor canon Crisparkle, and that clergyman's bond with Tartar, the "old fag" (243) of his school days. That Jasper and Neville are both painfully in love with Rosa, while Edwin is betrothed to her by paternal arrangement, and that Tartar (we assume) must eventually marry her objectify Rosa within this complicated power play as a signifier of masculine desire. For this reason, perhaps, her own nascent critique of a practice of domination can be too easily missed or dismissed as a petulant outburst. Rosa's objection, however, seems an important one to foreground in a novel persistently connecting masculine with imperial power. A faithful servant of both, Miss Twinkleton alternately "bore[s] about" Belzoni's unsuccessful explorations into pyramids and "fraudulent[ly]" edits Rosa's novels of unbridled romance into tracts of a middle-class domesticity. ("Ever engaged to me with the consent of our parents on both sides . . . let me call upon thy papa . . . and propose a suburban establishment . . . where every arrangement shall invest economy . . . with the attributes of the ministering angel to domestic bliss" [263]).

Miss Twinkleton performs complementary educational tasks necessary for the provision of competent wives and mothers to empire. "Oh you gentlemen, you gentlemen!" the harassed educator exclaims, "you are so hard upon us poor maligned disciplinarians of our sex, for your sakes" (117). The power relations explicit in her complaint are only a casual indication of the complicated imperial and sexual tensions interrogated in Dickens' last novel. The following pages read the negotiation of these tensions in their increasing complexity and suggest that these finally account for the narrative inconclusiveness of *Edwin Drood.*

❧

Dickens had long been interested in empire's impact on the domestic life of the metropolis. Almost twenty years before *Edwin
Drood,* while completing *Dombey and Son* and *David Copperfield,* he
had planned a new work "in which civilized men, under circumstances of difficulty, soonest become like savages" (E. Johnson
1979:356). Perhaps unsurprisingly, this mid-Victorian *Heart of
Darkness* failed to materialize. The idea, however, was to return in
more complex form in *Edwin Drood,* the narrative of a civilization
contaminated to its very core by outlandish savageries:

> An ancient English Cathedral Town? How can the ancient English
> Cathedral town be here! . . . What IS the spike that intervenes, and
> who has set it up? Maybe it is set up by the Sultan's orders for the
> impaling of a horde of Turkish robbers, one by one. It is so, for the
> cymbals clash, and the Sultan goes by to his palace. . . . Ten thou-
> sand scimitars flash in the sunlight and thrice ten thousand dancing
> girls strew flowers. Then, follow white elephants. . . . Still, the Ca-
> thedral tower rises in the background, where it cannot be, and still
> no writhing figure is on the spike. (37)[5]

These opening lines of *Edwin Drood* introduce "the ancient English Cathedral town" of Cloisterham through a sequence of incriminating mediations: in a vision that is the stuff of orientalist
fantasy, engendered on a filthy London bed shared "not longwise,
[with] . . . a Chinaman, a Lascar, and a haggard woman" (37) by a
dreamer just emerging from an opium hallucination. The vision's
associations are too shocking to be conceivable ("How can the
ancient English Cathedral town be here . . . where it cannot be"),
but they are cumulatively confirmed by the relentless trajectory of
the novel. In this presentation, Dickens' tainted metropolis does
indeed become the center of an anatomy of evil, caught in a
criminal exchange with the empire of which it is an integral part.

If *Edwin Drood* suggests that the increasing savagery of English
domestic life is a product of the imperial connection, the register
of that guilty relation is opium, a commodity made globally available only through the workings of the imperial system, while that
system depends for its viability on promoting opium consumption
anywhere *outside* its own metropolis. Such was the logic activating
the opium wars in the middle years of the century—wars in which
the English navy, first alone and then jointly with France, made
successive assaults on Chinese ports to open the way for Europe's
drug trade.[6]

A system of intricate moral discriminations had to be maintained to justify this Victorian narco-terrorism. The historian and liberal M.P. George Otto Trevelyan wrote scathingly of the government-run opium industry in *Competition Wallah:*

> What a book might be made of "The Confessions of an English Opium Agent." It is the most romantic of manufactures! Everywhere the drowsy scent of poppy . . . lulls the pleased visitor into a . . . sweet oblivion of the principles of competition and free trade. That little lump of black putty . . . bought a few days ago at forty pence . . . beneath the magic touch of the government becomes an equivalent for a sovereign. . . . Regard with awe those dark sticky globes, lying so snugly in their bed of kindred straw! These are cannon balls to extract tribute from the stranger!
>
> (1866:57)[7]

More recently, Kiernan wryly noted the moral contortions required by the Victorian drug trade:

> A Briton who smoked opium in India would have been guilty of a derogation only less unpardonable than a native wife; [though] he could drink unlimited whiskey to float him through . . . years of exile, because whiskey was not a native product. It was another odd differential that John Bull, the strange convolutions of whose conscience have never been fully anatomized, did not sell opium to his own Indian subjects; he dumped it on the Chinese, for whose vices he was not responsible. Envious of his opium profits and more logical, the French made opium a government monopoly in Indochina and sold it to the public for revenue.
>
> (1986:96–97)

The impact of opium on metropolitan life and morals, however, could not be completely ignored. In *Sybil* (1845), Disraeli's new candidate for parliament is "one McDruggy, fresh from Canton with a million of opium in each pocket, denouncing corruption and bellowing free trade" (1984:74). Ruskin displays great indignation in *Sesame and Lilies* (1865) that men who had made fortunes trading opium in the empire were free to buy estates at home in *England.* Though a web of infinitesimal distinctions might camouflage England's drug trafficking for all practical purposes, an acknowledgment of the centrality of opium to empire nevertheless emerged, in displaced and disguised form, in writing less directly concerned with the management of imperial proprieties. One such instance is this classic passage of nineteenth-century prose:

Some of these rambles led me to great distances: for an opium-eater is too happy to observe the motion of time. And sometimes in my attempt to steer homewards ... by fixing my eye on the pole star, and seeking ambitiously for a north-west passage, instead of circum-navigating all the capes and headlands I had doubled in my outward voyage, I came suddenly upon such knotty problems of alleys, such enigmatical entries and such sphinx's riddles of streets. ... I could almost have believed, at times, that I must be the first discoverer of some of these *terrae incognitae*. ... For all this, however, I paid a heavy price in distant years, when the human face tyrannized over my dreams ... with the feeling of perplexities moral or intellectual, that brought confusion to the reason, or anguish and remorse to the conscience (De Quincey 1971:81).

De Quincey's *Confessions of an English Opium Eater* (1822), osten-sibly a project of personal exploration and introspective psychic adventure, is read here as a signal text of English imperialism. This narrative of penniless, opium-driven explorations in the sphinx-ridden alleys of London might dislocate some nineteenth-century certainties, but if De Quincey deliberately declasses as well as ra-cially and sexually attaints himself by his wanderings, the coloniz-ing voyage is still the true paradigm of his vagrant expeditions. For De Quincey, opium *is* empire, conferring the same classic delusions: of power to invent new worlds, of denying any but his own time and space, of an untroubled priority. In addition, these ambitious voyages—internal and external, "both in a solid and a liquid shape ... both East-India and Turkey" (1971:92)—are si-multaneously expeditions into the uncharted back ways of home, all three forays equally fraught with guilt and threatening retribu-tion.

If the imperialist was, of necessity, the true opium addict, this knowledge not only had to remain concealed in imperial policy but also had to be displaced through skillful projection. Martin Bernal has connected the Victorians' increasing vilification of China with the exigencies of the opium trade: "The need to justify these actions and exploitation ... led to a transformation of the Western image of China. From being a model of rational civilization, China became seen as a filthy country in which torture and corruption of all sorts flourished. With obscene irony, the Chinese were espe-cially blamed for their consumption of opium" (1987:238).[8] The transference that enabled a generic "John Chinaman" to be con-structed as the ultimate opium addict is miniaturized in a bizarre episode of *Confessions*. De Quincey describes the sudden arrival of a man, assumed to be a Malay sailor, at Grasmere (that locus of profoundly English pastoral tranquility, inexorably the site of this classic scene of empire).[9] Englishman and Asian can discover no common language, but De Quincey offers the visitor a "piece of opium":

> To him, as an Orientalist, I concluded that opium must be familiar. ... Nevertheless I was struck with some little consternation when I saw him ... bolt the whole.... The quantity was enough to kill three dragoons and their horses: and I felt some alarm for the poor creature: but what could be done? ... I could not think of violating the laws of hospitality, by having him seized and drenched with an emetic.... For some days I felt anxious: but as I never heard of any Malay being found dead, I became convinced that he was used to opium.
>
> (91–92)

The grotesque logic of orientalism ensures that this "Malay" (quite possibly murdered by English "laws of hospitality") is recast as the secret opium fiend. Years later he returns as the aggressor, to "run amuck" through De Quincey's drugged imagination[10]:

> The Malay has been a fearful enemy for months. I have been every night, through his means, transported into Asiatic scenes. I know not whether others share in my feelings ... but I have often thought that if ... I were compelled to ... live in China ... I should go mad.... Southern Asia, in general is the seat of awful images.... In China ... I am terrified by the modes of life, by the manners, and the barrier of utter abhorrence ... placed between us by feelings deeper than I can analyze.... I ran into pagodas: and was fixed, for centuries, at the summit, or in secret rooms ... I fled from the wrath of Brama through all the forests of Asia.... I came suddenly upon Isis and Osiris: I had done a deed, they said, which the ibis and the crocodile trembled at. I was buried, for a thousand years ... with mummies and sphinxes, in narrow chambers at the heart of eternal pyramids. I was kissed, with cancerous kisses ... and laid, confounded with all unutterable slimy things, amongst ... Nilotic mud.
>
> (108–9)

The "Malay" initiates De Quincey into a vision that is the essence of orientalist fantasy: stock images of China, Egypt, and India merge with dreams of penetrating the "secret rooms" and "narrow chambers" of subject cultures. Like Rosa's boring archaeologist, the dreamer is almost entombed in the pyramids (perhaps as Edwin, another Egyptian doer, will be in the crypts of Cloisterham).

In these dreams De Quincey, like Jasper, has "done a deed" that dissolves his English identity and entraps him in a horrifying sequence of "oriental" activities—for opium, construed as the property of the conquered other, must inevitably compromise its white users. In the first chapters of *Edwin Drood*, Jasper is already orientalized by its excesses into a "jaded traveller" (39), an Englishman gone native at the very heart of empire. Embracing the "unclean spirit of imitation" (39) lodged in opium, Jasper succumbs indiscriminately to the degraded ways of Chinese, Turks, and Lascars. These ways, of which opium is the signifier, encompass a whole spectrum of "oriental" "vices," among them effeminacy, homosexuality, and "thuggee."

Sedgwick's suggestive essay "Up the Postern Stair" has placed *Edwin Drood* alongside the narratives of Richard Burton and T. E. Lawrence, imperial adventurers who produce male homosexuality as an oriental, and particularly Middle Eastern, practice.[11] This displacement (like the disavowal of opium) was an act of self-preservation; the ramifications for the imperialist who could admit such interior explorations are neatly summed up by Sedgwick: "Rosa may munch serenely on her sticky Turkish Lumps-of-Delight Candy; but for the English male, there is more at stake in Turkish pleasures. At stake, for instance . . . is a sultanly habit of impaling men on spikes" (189). Impaling and being impaled, the twin jeopardies of brutality and passivity fused in this construction of male homosexuality, are manifested in Jasper's other acquired attributes—effeminacy and the violence attendant on "thuggee."

"Thuggee" had come into English popular consciousness in the 1830s, when British officials reported having discovered a sect of murderers who lived by ritual strangulation of highway travelers according to the rites of the goddess Kali.[12] Irregular judicial methods (such as new trial procedures and previously inadmissible rules of evidence) were deemed necessary for its suppression. W. H. "Thuggee" Sleeman, an administrator responsible for many "thug" convictions, published a sensationalized account of his experiences that took immediate hold on the Victorian imagination. Sleeman's work was followed by much literary interest in "thuggee": De Quincey was fascinated by it; Bulwer-Lytton suggested a "Thug romance" to a retired colonial official, Meadows Taylor, who published his *Confessions of a Thug* in 1839. Taylor's work, described by Brantlinger as "one of the great Victorian crime novels" (1988:87) was extremely successful. In the 1860s, literary interest in "thuggee" was revived by Wilkie Collins' *The Moonstone,* which derives its gang of sinister Indian stranglers from Taylor. For years critics, including Edmund Wilson, have suggested that Dickens follows Collins in centering *Edwin Drood* around a "thuggee" murder.[13]

An "oriental" attribute, "thuggee" immediately feminizes its practitioners. Edmund Wilson supports his case for a "thuggee" connection in *Edwin Drood* by describing Jasper as "having 'thick, lustrous, well-arranged black hair and whiskers' and a voice that sometimes sounds 'womanish'—in short very much like a Hindu" (1941:87).[14] Wilson's chauvinist baggage hardly needs comment here; more significant is the complementary process by which Jasper is equally feminized and orientalized by opium, "thuggee," and implied homosexuality—a process encapsulated in the brilliant deployment of the single word *jaded.* Jasper is "womanish" because he has jaded himself out with "oriental" activities; concurrently, the "un-English complexion" he shares with Neville Landless is the outer signification of an unmanly (jadish) temperament.[15]

Woman and "Chinaman" are Jasper's jading Others, the contending fellow-travelers of his opium voyages. Princess Puffer, the mysterious "hostess" of the den who has "opium-smoked herself into a strange likeness of the Chinaman" (38), acknowledges this antagonistic affiliation: "Well, there's land customers and there's water customers. I'm a mother to both. Different from Jack Chinaman t'other side of the court. He ain't a father to neither. It ain't in him" (266). But Princess Puffer's feeling for Jasper is more complicated than maternal solicitude. The two share a mysterious bond compounded by his suspicious contempt and her profound, silent hatred, though the nature of their hidden relationship is never identified.

If the princess' individual story remains unplayed in the last, secret chapters of *Edwin Drood,* her history is less unknowable, figured compulsively in literature's need to absorb the displaced "fallen woman" within the plots of an upwardly mobile, self-consolidating society. The princess' history is inscribed clearly enough in De Quincey's text, in a passage bearing a strange resemblance to the opening fantasy of Dickens' novel:

> I thought that it was a Sunday morning in May. . . . I was standing
> . . . at the door of my own cottage [at Grasmere]. . . . The scene was
> an Oriental one; and there also it was Easter Sunday. . . . And at a
> vast distance were visible, as a stain upon the horizon, the domes
> and cupolas of a great city. . . . And not a bow-shot from me, upon
> a stone . . . there sat a woman; and I looked; and it was—Ann! . . .
> I waited: but she answered me not a word. Her face was the same as
> when I saw it last, and yet again how different! Seventeen years ago,
> when the lamp-light fell upon her face, as for the last time I kissed
> her lips (lips, Ann, that to me were not polluted) her eyes were
> streaming with tears.
>
> (111–12)

The vision expresses De Quincey's remorse over the sixteen-year-old "walker of the streets" (50) who befriended him and whom he "accidentally" abandoned in the course of his explorations in other London alleys. Jasper's hallucination, like De Quincey's, merges rural England and its reassuring Christian trappings with a superimposed panorama of troubling oriental splendor. But the central figure of De Quincey's dream is dispersed among the titillating forms of unnamed "dancing girls" fantasized by Jasper. The missing figure in Jasper's vision is a lost woman (forgotten, abandoned, unrepresentable), displaced from memory, a woman absent except for her unrecognized presence on the same contaminated bed.

Princess Puffer is Jasper's "fellow traveller" in ways unsuspected by him: she shares the opium bed, prepares his pipes, and manipulates his visions, all the while watching, listening, searching. "There was a fellow traveller, deary" (270) she warns when he returns to the den after the fatal journey of Edwin's disappearance. Jasper, missing the threat, applies the hint to Edwin, convinced that his "hostess" is too gross to make any journeys on her own account. "What visions can *she* have?" he asks contemptuously, "Visions of many butchers' shops, and public houses and much credit? Of an increase of hideous customers, and this horrible bedstead set upright again . . .? What can she rise to, under any quantity of opium, higher than that?" (38).

But the princess is envisioning revenge, forearmed even in sleep:

"As he falls, the Lascar . . . draws a phantom knife. It then becomes apparent that the woman has taken possession of his knife . . . for, she too starting up . . . the knife is visible in her dress, not in his, when they drowsily drop back, side by side" (39). Armed with her knowledge of the plot's secret, but cheated of the occasion for its disclosure, a lost woman displaced from memory (Jasper's, the text's, the reader's), Princess Puffer inhabits a space just beyond representation. Nameless except for a title that travesties her power and suggests unnamed degradations, she is approached only indirectly, through the hints and drugged nightmares in scripts of male exploration. The sphinx of London backways, her face, one of other faces, returns to "tyrannize over" their journeyings with a menace bringing "confusion to the reason, or anguish and remorse to the conscience" (De Quincey 1971:81).

The last pages of *Edwin Drood* establish Princess Puffer at the heart of Cloisterham Cathedral where, unlike the hallucinating Jasper or De Quincey, she remains unmoved by the icons of a contaminated Christianity: "As ugly and withered as one of the fantastic carvings . . . as malignant as the Evil one, as hard as the big brass eagle holding the sacred books upon his wings (and, according to the sculptor's presentation of his ferocious attributes, not at all converted by them), she hugs herself in her lean arms" (279). As the novel ends, Dick Datchery, observing her, can return home to chalk a thick score against Jasper's name; Princess Puffer, in Dickens' "presentation of [her] ferocious attributes," remains an unnamed fist-shaking figure, auguring a powerful but unfulfilled vengeance for unknown crimes. His text will comprehend *her* journey no further.

⌘

A second face tyrannizing De Quincey's opium voyages, his "fearful enemy," the "Malay" sailor, returns to haunt Dickens' novel in an unlikely manifestation: that of agitating, radical "philanthropists" who "run amuck like so many mad Malays" (207) in their violent opposition to the excesses of empire. The comparison is made by the worthy but thick-headed Canon Crisparkle during his hard-hitting argument with the "gunpowderous" do-gooder, Mr. Honeythunder.

This chapter's unusual vehemence was noted by K. J. Fielding (1952), who suggests that Honeythunder strongly resembles the radical M.P. John Bright, while several of the chapter's unexplained allusions refer to the Eyre controversy, still a source of bitter public debate in 1869.[16] The first of several administrative massacres in the British empire, the case involved the execution, at Governor Eyre's orders, of hundreds of Jamaicans in a violent response to their demand for reform. Liberals and radicals, including Bright's fellow members of Parliament Richard Cobden and John Stuart Mill, had called for Eyre's prosecution for murder.[17] The novel recapitulates Honeythunder's politics in language reminiscent of the attacks on Mill's Jamaica Committee: "You were to abolish military force, but you were first to bring all commanding officers who had done their duty, to trial by court martial for that offence, and shoot them. . . . You were to have no capital punishment, but were first to sweep off the face of the earth all legislators, jurists, and judges, who were of the contrary opinion. . . . Above all things you were to do nothing in private or on your own account. You were to go to the offices of the Haven of Philanthropy . . . and were ever more to live upon the platform" (85–86). The novel's clinching allusion to the Eyre controversy is a stinging pun developing the pugilistic tone set in the chapter's title: "Preparations were in progress for a moral little Mill [*sic*] somewhere on the rural circuit, and other Professors were backing this or that Heavy-weight as good for such or such speech-making hits" (201). Here, Mill, Cobden, Bright, and their reforming supporters at Exeter Hall become "Professors of the Noble art of fisticuffs," using the unfair means of platform speeches and public committees to attack faithful servants of empire.

Neither of the chapter's submerged references to the Eyre case, nor its attacks on Mill and his Exeter Hall supporters, are gratuitous: they pursue questions about the practice of empire raised persistently in other parts of the text. The public argument generated by the Eyre case can be summed up in a single concern— the nature of the necessary relationship between domestic and imperial actions. Was Eyre to be held as accountable for black lives and rights as he would have been for white? Did the imposition of martial law in Jamaica or Ireland set a precedent for introducing martial law in England? Could the excesses committed for empire return to tyrannize the metropolis that had engendered them?[18] If Dickens' public answer was no, declared in his deliberate support for Eyre, *Edwin Drood* poses the Eyre question in other disturbing forms: Can the opium habit induced in "Jack Chinaman" and a bunch of anonymous Lascars infect the sweet-voiced choirmaster of Cloisterham?[19] Can Edwin's lordly racial aggression explain the conflict between him and Rosa or account for "something radically amiss in the terms on which they had been gliding towards a life-long bondage" (166)? The text's answers to these questions remain equivocal and (deliberately?) incomplete.

A similar ambiguity characterizes Neville's trial by prejudice. The public's unfounded suspicions of Neville for Edwin's murder are heightened by the discovery that "before coming to England Neville had caused to be whipped to death sundry 'Natives'. . . vaguely supposed in Cloisterham to be always black, always of great virtue" (198). But if Neville, like Eyre, is the colonial settler who "understands how to treat Natives" and is persecuted for it by an obtusely liberal public at home, blind English jingoism is shown to be equally stupid and dangerous. Mr. Sapsea, characterized as an "old Tory Jackass" in Dickens' plans for the novel, is suspicious of Neville's "un-English complexion" (284), and "when Mr Sapsea has once declared anything to be un-English, he considers that thing everlastingly sunk in the bottomless pit" (180). Sapsea is the ultimate armchair imperialist, whose mastery—like Dombey's—is based on possessing the objects of empire:

> "If I have not gone to foreign countries, young man, foreign countries have come to me. They have come to me in the way of business. . . . I see some cups and saucers of Chinese make, equally strangers to me personally: I put my finger on them, then and there, and I say 'Pekin, Nankin, and Canton.' It is the same with Japan, with Egypt, and with bamboo and sandal-wood from the East Indies; I put my finger on them all."
>
> (64)

Jasper, who has his own ways of putting a finger on China or the East Indies, easily manipulates Sapsea: he serves him "genuine George the Third home-brewed; exhorting him (as 'my brave boys') to reduce to a smashed condition all other islands but this island, and all continents, peninsulas, isthmuses . . . and other geographical forms of land soever, besides sweeping the seas in all directions. In short, he rendered it pretty clear that Providence made a distinct mistake in originating so small a nation of hearts of oak, and so many other verminous peoples" (147–48). Although Jasper might gratify Sapsea's jingoism (the two drink confusion to the French, recalling the colonizing powers' rival interests in Egypt, China, and elsewhere), he has already secretly chosen that patriot's

monument to self-aggrandizement as a fit receptacle for the mold-
ering corpse of another staunch imperialist, Edwin himself.

If Honeythunder and Sapsea represent the extreme positions
on English imperial destiny, a more reassuring mean is suggested
by Tartar, a character poised between Edwin's Anglo-Saxon
bumptiousness and Neville's un-English air of being "the object
. . . of the chase" (85) rather than a pursuer: "A handsome gentle-
man, with a young face, but with an older figure in its robustness
and its breath of shoulder . . . so extremely sunburnt that the
contrast between his brown visage and the white forehead . . .
would have been almost ludicrous but for his . . . . bright blue eyes"
(214). A mix of white and brown, just redeemed from ludicrous-
ness by his boyish looks, Tartar belongs to an older breed of
empire builder. Edwin is the new-fashioned imperialist who will
"go engineering into the East," the ambitious expert impatient "to
wake up Egypt a little" (or to "open the eyes of John Chinaman");
the system has outgrown its need of muscular schoolboys like
Tartar. "Bred in the Royal navy" (215), Tartar's voyages, unlike
Jasper's, are all "seafaring" (266) and all safely over. Like William
Price, that good-natured sailor of an earlier era, he will be assimi-
lated into the landed gentry by an inheritance from a rich uncle.
His colonial experience will rigidify into reverently preserved,
meaningless shapes resembling the actual baggage brought out of
it: "Stuffed, dried, repolished . . . according to their kind . . . rep-
tiles, arms, articles of dress, shells . . . each was displayed in its
especial place. . . . Paint and varnish seemed to be kept somewhere
out of sight, in constant readiness to obliterate stray finger marks.
. . . No man of war was kept more spick and span from careless
touch" (248).

But however obsessive the preservation of empire's artifacts
from the dust and stains of history, inner deterioration is not to be
staved off. The weight of the "long-term cultural damage" empire
inflicts on its own center has been discussed by Ashis Nandy:

> The experience of colonizing did not leave the internal culture of
> Britain untouched. It began to bring into prominence those parts of
> the British political culture which were least tender and humane. It
> de-emphasized speculation, intellection and *caritas* as feminine, and
> justified a limited cultural role for women—and femininity. . . . It
> openly sanctified—in the name of such values as competition,
> achievement, control and productivity—new forms of institutional-
> ized violence and social Darwinism. The instrumental concept of the

lower classes it promoted was . . . only a slightly modified version of the colonial concept of hierarchy. . . . The tragedy of colonialism was also the tragedy of the younger sons, the women, and all "the etceteras and-so-forths" of Britain.

(1983:32)

Nandy's analysis captures the quality of Edwin's contempt for all those outside the privileged "doing, working, engineering" classes of empire: the scholarly and un-English Neville, the "womanish" musician Jasper, and Rosa, a "little goose" who "hates boilers." But the tragic rejects of the imperial process can also imitate its characteristic violence. Eyre's bureaucratic murders and the extralegal measures used against "thuggee" can be balanced against that cult's organized destructiveness or Princess Puffer's calculated program of retribution. Edwin's strangulation by the jaded and jadish Jasper is, in this sense, a cultural avenging—the turning of the stifled underside of empire upon itself. Jasper's real, if sexually repressed, love for Edwin decrees that the murder is also self-murder, an unavoidable consequence of the double life of the Victorian imperialist—the opium fiend who repudiates opium; the sexually repressed figure who dominates and debases its objects of desire; the respectable Christian who depends for a living on a thievish practice of "thuggee."

The faintly comic wholesomeness of Tartar and his runner-beans, or even the *Stalky and Co.* adventures implied by his naval past, hardly provide a serious counterweight to the sinister forces overrunning the novel's metropolis. England is represented by an opium-ridden London and a death-ridden Cloisterham saturated with the remains of past and present corpses; both locations are the scene of profound moral corruption. *Edwin Drood,* last in a sequence of Christmas novels, conjures no ghosts of past Dickensian jollities. Instead, its presiding spirit is the alien goddess Kali, invoked in this orientalist incarnation as the patroness of murder and destroyer of travelers. As described by the Victorian diarist Fanny Parks, Kali—a black, bloodied, and blatantly sexual figure —represents a punitive incarnation of the repressed:

The goddess is represented as a black female with four arms. . . . In one hand she carries a scymitar; in two others the heads of giants, which she holds by the hair. . . . Her tongue hangs down to her chin. The heads of giants are hung as a girdle around her loins, and her jet black hair falls to her heels. Having drunk the blood of the

giants she slew, her eyebrows are bloody, and the blood is falling in
a stream down her breast. . . . She stands with one leg on the breast
of her husband Shivu, and rests the other on his thigh.

(1850:1:165)

If, as Wilson and other critics have argued, *Edwin Drood* tells the
story of its hero's murder by Kali's sacred rites in the precincts of
Cloisterham Cathedral on Christmas Eve, that telling must mark a
crucial moment of transition.[20] In an 1837 review of "Thuggee"
Sleeman's memoirs, Charles Trevelyan summed up Kali's embodiment of all that was most inimical to Victorian values by asserting:
"If we were to form a graduated scheme of religions, that of Christ
and Kalee would be the opposite extremes" (quoted, Sleeman
1971:38). In this context, the celebration of Kali's destructive presence in Cloisterham must be read as a signal of the final inconceivable merging of boundaries between metropolis and empire, a
fulfillment of the novel's opening fantasy of the cathedral protected by impaling spikes—the Eyre question answered in horri-
fyingly decisive form. Such a decisive conclusion, however, is precisely what the novel withholds, permanently. *Edwin Drood* ends
abruptly with its author's death, leaving the secret of its pivotal
murder undisclosed. The final scene, slightly less inconceivable,
substitutes Princess Puffer for Kali, an orientalized London sphinx,
shaking both fists at Jasper in Cloisterham Cathedral. With the
ambiguity that has been characteristic throughout, her gesture
passes almost unnoticed except by another mysterious, falsely named
observer.

The corruptions of empire—the consequences of its passion for
"doing," the sexual and political repercussions of its racial arrogance, the internal dissensions engendered by the opium trade
and by the institutionalized violence of the Eyre case—return to
tyrannize *Edwin Drood* with a variety of faces. These are the alien
countenances of generic Lascars, "mad Malays," and "Jack Chinaman"; the distorted features of a Princess Puffer; and, finally,
unmentioned and unmentionable, the visage of Kali, that absolute
Other who frighteningly encompasses all the most repressed attributes of empire itself.

Balanced against these are familiar faces: the angular but
shrewdly benevolent Grewgious, the generous Crisparkle, and Rosa,
energized into unusual resourcefulness by the inspiring friendship
of Helena Landless. Helena, her "tigerish" antecedents tempered
by native integrity, is the unknown factor of the novel, perhaps

presiding over its last pages, a kind of benign Kali disguised in the form of Dick Datchery.[21] In his introduction to the Penguin edition of *Edwin Drood,* Angus Wilson asserts that this would be a "peculiarly un-Dickensian" maneuver (1986:19–20), but Helena *is* a new heroine for Dickens—dynamic, decisive, intrepid. Her name recalls the love of Dickens' last years, Ellen Lawless Ternan, and his fictional Estella—both women who refused to be contained by the domestic roles assigned to Dickens' earlier heroines. True to the rhythm already established, however, Helena's success is never realized in the novel. What remains—the determined rectitude of Crisparkle, Grewgious, and Tartar, the relentless detective skills of "Datchery," and Princess Puffer—seems to count for little against the public evils of Sapsea and Honeythunder or the profound psychic damage evidenced by Jasper.

Edwin Drood's incompleteness, then, only highlights a constitutional indeterminacy. But *could* the novel ever deliver a "Dickensian" conclusion that would transplant a happy Rosa Bud to Tartar's garden-in-the-air, or unite Helena's splendid energy with the unmitigated decency of the minor canon?[22] Could the faces that haunt its criminal metropolis metamorphose into more benign forms, like the Roman dead in whose remains "Cloisterham children grow small salad" (50)? An England cleansed as spotless as Tartar's lodgings "that you might have supposed the London blacks emancipated forever, and gone out of the land for good" (247)? For all Tartar's scrubbing, London's fog remains; "A Gritty State of Things Comes On" (247) once more, despite the hopeful title of the next—and final—chapter.

Some twenty years later, many of the constituent elements of *Edwin Drood*—the disintegration of its marriage plot and hints of secret homosexual desire, concern with the destructive aspects of the artist-figure, fascination with the debaucheries of opium and orientalism, patterns of return and the fallen woman's retribution—are successfully combined and resolved, not in the realistic novel but in the very different narrative form of Oscar Wilde's latter-day Gothic fable, *The Picture of Dorian Grey.* Deprived of the supernatural consolations of Wilde's book, Dickens' text throughout chooses incompleteness over closure, fragment over final testament—the least threatening resolution, perhaps, of the frightening processes of domination and retribution inscribed in its pages.

Where *Belinda,* the first text considered in this study, ended with its disruptive marginal voices contained by external "improvements," I have suggested that the difficulty of containing these frightening presences finally accounts for the incompleteness of *Edwin Drood.* In its last pages, many of the tensions of empire outlined in the various chapters of this study become thoroughly internalized, brought home as sexual and economic tensions to overrun an ancient English cathedral town. Within the mainstream of the novel genre in the decades after 1870, empire no longer functions as a suggestive hidden presence but becomes an explicit force shaping both the search for appropriate form in Schreiner's *The Story of an African Farm* (1883) and the pervasive worldly ironies of James or Conrad. The unfinished *Edwin Drood,* with its fusion of anxieties, may be seen as a particularly significant marking of the process of transition between the two stages.

❧

Conclusion

Don't talk to me about Matisse, don't talk to me
about Gauguin, or even
the earless painter Van Gogh
& the woman reclining on a blood spread . . .
the aboriginal shot by the great white hunter Matisse
with a gun with two nostrils, the aboriginal
crucified by Gauguin—the syphilis spreader, the yellowed obesity.

Don't talk to me about Matisse . . .
the European style of 1900, the tradition of the studio
where the nude woman reclines forever
on a sheet of blood.

Talk to me instead of the culture generally—
how the murderers were sustained
by the beauty robbed of savages: to our remote
villages the painters came, and our white washed
mud-huts were splattered with gunfire.
                              —LAKDASA WIKKRAMASINHA,
                              "DONT TALK TO ME ABOUT MATISSE"

*I*N A sustained consideration of the "placing," or contextualiz-
ing of, an artistic tradition, Raymond Williams makes an extremely
important qualification about the need to balance two sorts of
judgment within any kind of revisionist enterprise. Discussing his
critique of the country-house tradition in *The Country and the City,*
Williams tells his interlocutors in *Politics and Letters:*

There is one level at which we can say that a specific form was
historically productive and therefore historically valuable—in that

sense it was a major contribution to human culture. But we must also be able to say, in a distinct but connected way, that it was a disastrously powerful contribution. . . . If you cannot make the first judgment, then all history becomes a current morality, and there ceases to be any history. If you cannot make the second, I do not know what an affiliation to the working class would be for me. . . . Of course, if you get to the second judgment without the first, the result becomes naïveté: you will not understand enough history to be able to locate yourself in it or to be morally offended by any part of it. On the other hand, if you don't feel offence at this profoundly conventional mystification [the writing out of the laborer in the country-house poetry of Ben Jonson] . . . then what is the meaning of solidarity?

(1981:307)

Williams' is an argument for detail, scholarship, differentiation, discrimination, and analysis in the formation of critical (in all the senses that word encompasses) judgments.

This patient outlining of the need for discrimination as well as judgment, and for careful contextualization as well as sensibility, seems especially pertinent today against the charged rhetoric, inflated claims, counterclaims, and dismissals that mystify any attempt to scrutinize the literary canon or its role in higher education (Hancock 1990). In an editorial published in the *Wall Street Journal*, for example, Bernard Lewis warns that the current debate over the "great books" curricula in U.S. universities is no less than a debate over the stability of Western culture.[1] For Lewis, disputing or dislocating the canon not only could lead to the return of slavery but also "would . . . facilitate the introduction of another almost universal non-Western institution: the harem. . . . In addition to polygamy and concubinage, other non-Western practices that might accompany this change [in college curriculum] could include child marriage and the burning of widows" (1988:24).

It is highly significant that Lewis invokes here many of the same orientalist constructions we have seen constituted, absorbed, and negotiated within the very books he and other champions of Western culture are anxious to retain in their present places in university curricula. Both the currency of the connection made here between the "non-Western" and "polygamy, . . . concubinage, . . . and the burning of widows" *and* the vision that sees the cultural texts of the West as the last line of defense against such "non-Western practices" depend to a large extent on the seemingly neutral status of these works, as well as on a belief in their ahistorical existence apart from their constitution in discourse. Tracing the construction, processing, absorption, and contestation of such formulations of "non-Western practices" within those very discourses and narrative forms that are taken to be most removed from and antithetical to them then becomes a key task in moving the argument beyond the level of assertions and rebuttals, denials and blanket rejections, to an understanding of the complex set of meanings generated by "great books."

While sharing Wikkramasinha's impulse to challenge "the European style of 1900" (1976:83), *Reaches of Empire* tries also to remain true to the set of critical requirements outlined by Williams, agreeing with Lewis and like-minded educators to this extent: that the canon of Western culture still needs to be read—but read within a newly available historical and cultural context, against both the oppositional and repressed voices of its own time (now being rediscovered in ever-increasing numbers) and the revisionist voices of present-day scholarship. In its attempt to reexamine one crucial (and for that reason sometimes overlooked) literary tradition among the many sets of "big volumes" within Western culture, it is my hope that this book illuminates and contributes to that necessary process of reading and rereading.

Notes

Preface

1. For similar comments, see Woolf 1961:25–26 and 151, and the letter to Lytton Stratchey, 47.

2. See Hancock's recent essay in the *Village Voice* (1990) for a recapitulation of this controversy.

Introduction: Reading Noncollusively

1. To name only a handful of examples, see Raskin 1971, Sandison 1967, Wurgaft 1983, Greenburger 1967, McClure 1981, and Jan-Mohamed 1983. A few essays do exist on empire in earlier nineteenth-century novels (for example, Said on *Mansfield Park* [1989], Spivak on *Frankenstein* and *Jane Eyre* [1985a], Meyer on *Jane Eyre* [1989]), but the only book-length study so far is Brantlinger's *Rule of Darkness* (1988), discussed later in this chapter.

2. See Marlowe's aspirations in the opening chapter of *Heart of Darkness* and Conrad's own similar feelings in the autobiographical essay "Geography and Some Explorers."

3. For a more recent and perhaps even more far-reaching reappraisal along the lines suggested by Green, see Street's 1985 essay on reclassifying the "Adventure Tale."

4. See, for example, Kucich's 1989 critique of Brantlinger's *Rule of Darkness*, 217.

5. A more complex view than Green's, closer to my own analysis, is also suggested by Daniell in an essay on Buchan's *Prester John:* "[In earlier decades] Empire can be seen as something as attractive as simply the extension of the family overseas. . . . Empire could, even in the mid–nineteenth century, mean exploration, or what was understood to be so, map-making, engineering, medicine, and special interests in literatures, languages and the problems of translation. Much of . . . this was inspired by, and often a part of, the growth of literature for children, without distinction of sex." By the end of the century, however, a change appears: popular literature "becomes aggressively, and defensively, imperialist. It leaves the Christian family ambience and becomes all-male and public school: military values invade and take over the stories" (1985:141).

6. Spenser's *A View of the Present State of Ireland* was written in 1596 and published in 1633.

7. Hulme's excellent chapter on *Robinson Crusoe* (1986) develops these connections in detail.

8. Carter's reference to the explorer's vocabulary repeatedly employed in Sterne's *Tristram Shandy* is also relevant here: "[Sterne] was the writer who . . . came nearest to transforming the narrative tradition of the novel into a map of passions. He . . . made capes of noses, passages of breeches . . . [and] could convince himself 'there is a North-west passage to the intellectual world' " (1988:200).

9. The influence of the oriental tale on the early Romantic poets, especially Byron and Southey, and on the Gothic novelists Mathew "Monk" Lewis and Ann Radcliffe is also discussed by Conant (1908).

It is significant that several nineteenth-century novelists (including Edgeworth, the Brontës, Dickens, and Thackeray) wrote or planned "oriental" tales or plays at some point in their careers. Conant cites Edgeworth's *Popular Tales* (1804), Thackeray's juvenilia and later short stories, and Dickens' youthful tragedy "Misnar, the Sultan of India," based on Ridley's *Tales of the Genii* (1764). The Brontës' early projects should also be included in this category.

10. Parry's characterization of literary discourse "as the *fount* of ideology or . . . initiating new modes of address to construct not-yet-existing conditions" (1987:50; emphasis added) is relevant here.

11. See, for example, Poovey's demonstration of the "mutual rhetorical construction" of Florence Nightingale's domestic campaign to establish nursing as a complete system of enlightenment within England and the midcentury representations of English rule as a health-bringing transfusion for India after the 1857 uprising (1988:194–99).

12. Woolf is less incisive on other occasions, however: *A Room of One's Own* maintains that "[Women] are not . . . as concerned about the health of their fame and . . . will pass a tombstone or a signpost without feeling an irresistible urge to cut their names on it, as Alf, Bert or Chas. must do in obedience to their instinct, which murmers if it sees a fine woman go

by, or even a dog, *Ce chien est à moi*. And, of course, it may not be a dog . . . it may be a piece of land or a man with curly black hair. It is one of the advantages of being a woman that one can pass even a very fine negress without wishing to make an Englishwoman of her" (1929:52). Woolf's absolution of "women" from any form of political responsibility and her failure to confront the relation between "woman," "negress," and "Englishwoman" in her last sentence suggest that the clarity of *Three Guineas* was achieved only late in her career.

13. For example, Schreiner's *Woman and Labour* (1911), a pioneering work of feminist theory, argues that the division of labor along gender lines, with the resultant marginalization of the "parasitic woman," is "based on another and yet larger social phenomenon; it has invariably been preceded . . . by the subjugation of large bodies of other human creatures, either as slaves, subject races, or classes. . . . It has invariably been by feeding on this wealth, the result of forced or ill paid labour, that the female of the dominant race or class has . . . lost her activity and come to exist purely through the passive performance of her sexual functions" (98). For both Schreiner and Woolf, the practices of dominating women interlock with and reinforce class and race domination.

On Butler, see Uglow's essay "From Sympathy to Theory" (1983:146–62).

14. "As a narrative pattern, the romance plot muffles the main female character [and] . . . incorporates individuals within couples as a sign of their personal and narrative success. The romance plot separates love and quest, values sexual asymmetry, including the division of labor by gender, is based on extremes of sexual difference, and evokes an aura around the couple itself. In short, the romance plot, broadly speaking, is a trope for the sex-gender system as a whole" (DuPlessis 1985:5).

15. "*Imperialism* developed as a word during the second half of C19. *Imperialist* is much older . . . but . . . it meant the adherent of an emperor or imperial form of government. *Imperial* itself, in the same older sense, was in English from C14. . . . *Imperialism,* and *imperialist* in its modern sense, developed primarily in English, especially after 1870" (R. Williams 1983b:159).

16. See Magdoff 1978 for a detailed consideration of the different phases of imperialism.

17. Fryer notes that *The Cambridge History of English Literature* describes Carlyle as "the strongest moral force in the literature of his time . . . [who] affirmed . . . the eternal needs for righteousness in the dealings of man with man" (1984:172). To cite an instance from among the most sensitive modern critics, Williams' chapter on Carlyle in *Culture and Society* makes no reference either to the essay or to the general racism of Carlyle's views (1983a:71–86). In *Politics and Letters,* Williams acknowledges this omission, with the less-than-complete explanation that he does not follow Carlyle beyond the late 1840s (1981:104–5).

Chapter 1. Interruption, Interpolation, "Improvement": Inscribing Abolition and "Amalgamation" in Edgeworth's Belinda

1. See Kelly, "Thus Thady's tale in effect argues for what it doesn't actually describe . . . a landed gentry with the professional training and self-discipline necessary for social leadership. . . . But if the model does not appear in the story of *Castle Rackrent*, it nevertheless appears in the text" (1989:77).

2. Asked by a white woman in the United States if she would support marriage between races, Martineau replied that she would "never . . . try to separate persons who really loved . . . but I observed that . . . I believed the blacks were no more disposed to marry the whites than the whites to marry the blacks. 'You are an amalgamationist!' cried she. I told her . . . she must give what name she pleased to the principle I had declared" (1969:1:229).

3. *Belinda* was in fact revised twice after publication: shortly after the appearance of the first (anonymous) edition in 1801 and again in 1810 for Anna Barbauld's collection. For a discussion of the first, less significant, set of changes, see Butler 1972:283–85 and 494–95.

4. See Dykes 1942:145 and Lorimer 1978:30–31. Hawthorne is one of the few literary critics to pay some attention to the change. Among the biographers, Clarke, who is usually disapproving of Richard Edgeworth's "lamentable intervention" (1949:28) in his daughter's works, thinks this particular change "not altogether unadvisedly" made (59).

5. Harriot's name has been the subject of some speculation. The earliest *OED* reference for *freak* in its current sense of "monstrosity" is 1847. The modern *freak* is a variant of the obsolete *freke*, which meant "one eager for fight, champion," or "poetic synonym for a man." This usage, however, was last recorded in 1604. In 1800, the word was synonymous with a "capricious humour" or "whim." Discussed in Atkinson and Atkinson 1984:100.

6. Popular unrest throughout the 1790s culminated in the peasant rising of 1798, accompanied by a French-led landing in County Mayo in August. The French came within a few miles of Edgeworthstown, and the family had to be briefly evacuated (Butler 1972:137).

7. For example, the stories of the legendary Maroon leader "Grandy Nanny," who was believed to have defeated several British armies with her magic (Bilby and Steady 1981:457–58) and of the burning at the stake in the 1730s of Sally Basset, a slave who later achieved legendary status, for being "the ringleader" of a poisoning plot (Ferguson 1987:29). For other accounts of female resistance see Craton 1982:132–33 and 260–61 and Dadzie 1990:32–34.

8. See Butler 1972:282 for a suggestion that some of the punishment originally intended for Lady Delacour was transferred to Harriot Freke's

character when a happy ending was substituted for the former's death from breast cancer.

9. The issue of Freke's ambiguous sexual status, referred to only in passing here, needs a separate discussion that would take into account her cross-dressing, her abduction of Miss Moreton, and her unsuccessful attempts to "abduct" and to gain moral mastery over Lady Delacour and Belinda.

10. Hannah More's 1808 novel *Coelebs in Search of a Wife* also features a feminist antiheroine who, like Freke, rides and drives like a man, attempts "intrepid" feats, and interrupts male conversations with her own forceful opinions (Johnson 1989:163).

11. The term *abolition* is used throughout in its original sense to apply equally to movements that sought an end to the slave trade and those that aimed at ending the institution of slavery itself.

12. Quoted, Fryer 1984:207. See also James 1963:50–53 and E. Williams 1972 on the relative unimportance of humanitarian agitation: "the abolition of the slave system was basically the result of the fact that the system had lost its former importance . . . to the metropolitan economy" (Williams 1972:280–81). See Fryer 1984:207–14 for a summary of the contributions of well-intentioned but ultimately ineffectual abolitionists. For accounts of individuals, including Day and Seward, see Dykes 1942:21–23.

13. "The Dying Negro" was typical of the sentimentality and extravagance associated with one strain of English philanthropy. As the title indicates, the movement had a marked preference for representations of slaves in supine, supplicant, or other prone and powerless positions (Jordan 1968; Dykes 1942).

14. Richard Edgeworth's phrase, quoted in Butler 1972:149. Day's anger when he heard about the proposed publication of her translation of Madame de Genlis dissuaded Richard Edgeworth from "turning Maria into an authoress." See also Clarke 1949:31. Day died in 1792. *Letters for Literary Ladies* appeared in 1795, *The Parent's Assistant* in 1796.

15. Edwards' 1985 essay is a valuable recent contribution on black antislavery writers during this period, but the most detailed works on this topic are still those of Dykes and Sypher, both completed in the 1940s.

16. I am grateful to Susan Heath for introducing me to Brunton's novel, newly reissued by Pandora Press.

17. See also Dabydeen's description of Wheatley's eighteenth-century portrait of a family group representing the black servant "at the edge of the picture and slightly to the back, spacially divided from the white aristocratic family. . . . Even the dog is more a part of the family's affections than the black, the dog being a central, not a peripheral detail. In fact blacks and dogs shared the same status in the aristocratic household" (1987:21).

18. On the emergence of Creoles as literary types, and their inevitable moral inferiority, see Sypher 1939. Creole women in particular seem to have been a favorite target long before Bertha Mason's now celebrated appearance in *Jane Eyre*.

19. Herbert Spencer, for example, suggested that "[English] women of inferior ranks" were like primitives in their thinking because they were "full of personal experiences," "inexact," "averse to precision," and "quickly form very positive beliefs" (quoted, Stocking 1987:229).

20. The original passage read: " 'Well, Lucy,' said Lady Anne, 'have you overcome your fear of poor Juba's black face?' The girl reddened, smiled and looked at her grandmother, who answered for her in an arch tone. 'O, yes, my lady! We are not afraid of Juba's black face now; we are grown very great friends' " (quoted, Hawthorne 1975:175).

21. Quoted by Dykes 1942:21. See also Sypher 1969:177–81. "The Dying Negro" was, in fact, coauthored with a schoolmate, Joseph L. Bicknell, though Edgeworth follows her contemporaries in attributing the entire poem to Day. Day's other well-known composition, *Sandford and Merton,* also features an African slave in love with a white maid servant.

22. According to Sypher in his study of abolitionist literature, "there were at least 14,000 Negro slaves in England" by 1807 (1969:3). Present-day estimates would probably be even higher.

23. Rousseau's views on women's education, which Day and Hervey put into practice, made the French thinker suspect with both pro- and anti-Revolution women writers. Wollstonecraft openly challenged Rousseau's prescription that "the education of women should be always relative to men" (Kirkham 1983:46). Edgeworth's dismissal of Rousseau's educational theories is, therefore, less a positive indication of anti-Jacobinism than a coded endorsement of Wollstonecraftian feminism.

24. Edgeworth's personal correspondence also suggests a shrewd understanding of her own later occupation as rent collector on the family estate in County Longford. Clarke's 1949 biography relates that Edgeworth's letters to her younger brother Pakenham, a civil servant in India, "told him . . . that many of the problems with which he had to deal in Cucherry [*sic*] were like those which in a small way came under her for settlement in Ireland. . . . She too had to settle disputes between boundaries . . . and she naturally sympathised with his generous indignation at any form of exploitation of the poor peasants" (154).

25. Frances Edgeworth's words, quoted in Butler 1972:418–19.

26. Johnson's toast to slave revolution, made "in the company of some very grave men at Oxford," is described in Boswell's *Life* (1953:876). (Boswell himself was a firm supporter of slavery and published his *No Abolition of Slavery* hoping to influence the parliamentary debate of 1791. For a discussion of Johnson's positions in various abolitionist debates, see Sypher 1969:58–60.)

Chapter 2. Proper Places: Spatial Economies in Austen and Gaskell

1. On "the *topos* of rural simplicity" in early nineteenth-century fiction, see Kelly 1989:87–92, and, more generally, R. Williams 1973.

2. The term *Greater Britain*, however, did not come into popular use until the last third of the century, when Charles Dilke chose it as the title of his 1868 book on empire.

3. See Dykes' 1942 study for a brief survey of Romanticism and abolition.

4. This is true even when European iniquity is presented through the naive exclamations of virtuous "orientals" as in some of Voltaire's satires. Such tales rely for their effect on the reversal of the governing expectation of Europe's moral authority. See also Kelly 1989:218–20 on a successful 1828 novel by the anglicized Persian diplomat James Morier, titled *The Adventures of Hajji Baba, of Ispahan, in England.*

5. The new emphasis on moral superiority is evident also in the shift from slave trading to a more respectable policy of empire. This shift is enacted in the successful career of the abolitionist James Stephen, who became under secretary for the colonies in 1836; significantly, Stephen's nickname, "Mr Mothercountry," encompasses both national consciousness and imperial responsibility.

6. See Mazlish 1973:116–54 for the dynamics of the family trinity created by James Mill and his twin "offspring," John Stuart Mill and British India.

7. Compare Jameson's discussion of the mapping of imperial connections as one of the formal characteristics of modernism. Jameson asserts that "the traces of imperialism can therefore be detected in Western modernism, and are indeed constitutive of it; but we must not look for them in the obvious places, in content or in representation" (1990:64). Although the first half of Jameson's statement is suggestively and persuasively supported by his essay, I would dispute both his claim that "traces of imperialism" are not detectable in the content or representation of modernism and his earlier formulation of "imperialism" to exclude any significant "traces" of it in literature prior to the period of "new imperialism."

8. Brantlinger has described the actions of the British Navy in these years as sometimes "closer to privateering" (1988:48) than to full-scale naval battles with the French. Among others, Martin Green has cited the biographical evidence—the naval careers of her brothers and the part played by one in the annexation of Burma—for Austen's increasing interest in the navy (1979:341–42).

9. Compare Musselwhite's description of *Mansfield Park:* "It is perhaps the major achievement of *Mansfield Park* to have broken with the values of

a waning rural order and to have replaced it by one better suited to the rigours of an imperial and industrial age. Fanny's piety and quietism, as well as her interest in the slave trade and Lord Macartney on China, are early examples of that censorious concernedness that will serve well as an apologetics for exploitation at home and imperial expansion abroad" (1987:23).

10. For a detailed reading of empire and *Mansfield Park,* see Said 1989. On the novel's linking of feminism and abolition, see Kirkham 1983. Deforest 1987 discusses abolition in relation to *Emma.*

11. See Poovey's related discussion of *David Copperfield,* 1988:114–16.

12. On the merchant as a glorious and civilizing figure in eighteenth-century literature, see Dabydeen 1985.

13. This naval subplot also suggests the widening horizons of the novel in the mid–nineteenth century and the literary impact of Captain Marryat's naval stories during the 1830s and 1840s. See Brantlinger 1988:47–70 for more on Marryat's tales, in which the midshipmen and lieutenants of Austen and Gaskell feature as central characters.

14. Irish laborers and immigrants occupy a complicated position in several "Condition-of-England" novels (Disraeli's *Sybil,* Kingsley's *Alton Locke*), both representing the greatest working-class suffering and yet exempt from sympathy because of their colonial and "racially" different status.

15. In the retrospective *Politics and Letters* (1981), however, Williams seems somewhat more aware of the differences between the two kinds of endings (118).

16. This is suggested by Williams himself in his declaration in *The Country and the City* that "from at least the mid-nineteenth century, and with important instances earlier, there was this larger context [empire] within which every idea and every image was consciously and unconsciously affected" (1973:281). It seems fair to say, however, that Williams' careful delineations of empire at work occur only in writing dealing with the period *after* 1870—for example, in the last chapters of *The Country and the City* or in *Orwell.* For a discussion of Williams and empire, see Said 1989:152–53.

17. For a measured discussion of Wakefield and his proposals, see Semmel 1970:82ff.

18. For eighteenth- and nineteenth-century ideas of the transformative effects of migration on the female character, see Summers' *Damned Whores and God's Police* (1975), an analysis of women migrants in Australia.

19. In some ways, Defoe's Moll Flanders is a prototype of these displaced or unnecessary women, though her development is somewhat different. See the discussion in Kenny 1984:90–96.

Chapter 3. "Wholesale, Retail, and for Exportation": Empire and the Family Business in Dombey and Son

1. The Narrative of the Expedition sent by her Majesty's Government to the River Niger in 1841, under the command of Captain H. D. Trotter, R.N., by Captain William Allen, R.N., and T. R. H. Thompson, M.D., "Published with the sanction of the Colonial Office and the Admiralty." All quotations are from Dickens' review "The Niger Expedition," which appeared in The Examiner on August 19, 1848, and is reprinted in Miscellaneous Papers.

2. This pressure to distinguish between the heartless and extravagant aristocratic woman and the "feminine" and loving Florence is evident in the persistent satire of Mrs. Skewton and her noble friends in Dombey and Son.

3. Exeter Hall, the center of abolitionist and missionary activity, is a favorite literary target throughout the mid-Victorian period. Godfrey Ablewhite, the hypocritical villain of Collins' The Moonstone (1868) is one of its most eloquent members. Carlyle dubbed Exeter Hall politics "rose-pink sentimentalism" in his "Occasional Discourses on the Negro Question" (1849); Disraeli attacked it in both Sybil (1845) and Tancred (1847). See also my chapter on Edwin Drood.

4. Temperley has shown that the critique of Mrs. Jellyby in Bleak House draws on arguments long familiar in "the standard defence of slavery" (1972:71–72) in both Britain and the United States.

5. Dombey and Son was written in installments from 1846 to March 1848. The first complete edition appeared later in 1848. The actual Expedition, its preparation, and aftermath were, of course, public events throughout the 1840s.

6. See Auerbach 1985:116 and Musselwhite 1978:208.

7. Compare Marx's linkage, in 1867, of the three key elements in Dickens' passage: "The colonial system ripened trade and navigation as in a hothouse. The 'Companies called Monopolia'. . . were powerful levers for the concentration of capital. The colonies provided a market for the budding manufactures, and a vast increase in accumulation which was guaranteed by the mother country's monopoly of the market. The treasures captured outside Europe by undisguised looting, enslavement, and murder flowed back to the mother-country and were turned into capital there" (1981:1:918).

8. For the autobiographical relevance of The Newcomes and a more general discussion of Thackeray's Indian background, see Brantlinger 1988:94–107.

9. "The magic word in which the different classes and strata seemed to converge was 'adventure.' The knightly adventure, the cooperative trade enterprise, the manly deed, the life of employees, of entrepreneurs who no longer went on trade journeys themselves, even the dangerous enterprise and the goods themselves—all went by the same name. . . . But

it would be a mistake to see only this magic key word and to overlook the ideological differences contained in the various ideological systems which seem to be united at this one point: the class antagonisms are only superficially concealed (if at all) in this word" (Nerlich 1987:1:133).

10. Mukherjee's classic study of mercantilism traces the career of the Company from its aggressive militarist phase (which was "not an accidental phenomenon but the consummation of the governing desire of merchant capital" [1974:39]) to its overthrow by the more cautious, seemingly pacifist, proponents of free-trade capitalism.

11. On the domestic upheaval wrought by the railway, electric telegraph, and other products of Victorian industrialization, see R. Williams' 1970 introduction to the Penguin edition of the novel.

12. Auerbach's reading seems to follow from her contention that "Unlike other overweening institutions in Dickens' novels—Chancery in *Bleak House,* or the Circumlocution Office in *Little Dorrit*—Dombey and Son is defined in terms that are sexual and metaphysical rather than social. It exists as a gigantic end, the source and destination of all motion, all order, the center not so much of its society as of its universe" (1985:112). I would argue that Auerbach's exclusion of empire as a *social* reality in the novel accounts for her reading of the firm of Dombey and Son as a primarily "sexual and metaphysical" concern.

13. Moynahan 1962 and Welsh 1986 also comment on the stifling and unhealthy nature of Florence's overwhelming love and the death she is constantly associated with, but they assign different values to it.

14. See also *Dombey and Son,* 267. Clark has noted the impact of the various free trade struggles of the 1840s, including the repeal of the Navigation and the Corn Laws, on the text—decisions that marked the triumph of industrial over agrarian interests and opened the world market to England's manufactured goods (1984:75–76).

15. For the impact of the Expedition's failure on the abolitionist movement and on the career of the famous abolitionist Thomas Buxton, see Temperley 1972:55–61.

16. Stokes identifies Free Trade, Evangelicalism, and Philosophic radicalism as the "constituent elements" of "English liberalism in its clear untroubled dawn" (1959:xiv). See Temperley 1972:68–82 for an examination of the complex drive behind this combination of high finance and religious conscience, profit motive and reformism, in the careers of two great banking and abolitionist families, the Buxtons and the Barclays.

17. In Bagstock and his attendant, Dickens revives an extinct species of colonial tradition, the bygone nabobs and absentee landlords recalled by Disraeli in *Sybil:* "the West Indies exhausted, and Hindostan plundered, the breeds died away, and now exist only in our English comedies from Wycherley and Congreve to Cumberland and Morton" (107).

18. Fryer quotes from a poem of the 1790s that describes dark servants as the "Index of Rank or Opulence Supreme" (1984:73). On blacks

as icons of wealth in commercial pageants, signs, and billboards, see Fryer 1984:29–30. For a general discussion of the colonial relationship produced in oil painting see Berger 1972:83–95. See Dabydeen 1987 for a detailed analysis of the representational meaning of black figures in eighteenth-century art.

19. Here the text contradicts Clark, who suggests that Dombey "seems improbably disinclined to invest or speculate" and who claims that "the text is so opaque about what Dombey actually does that we can only conjecture about his business dealings, but his mode of confronting the world is is essentially ungiving and unadventurous. Apart from the . . . occasional soiree of conspicuous consumption . . . Dombey's austerity provides an upper class version of Scrooge's miserliness" (1984:76). As I suggest throughout this chapter, Dombey's "prodigious ventures" in the empire are invisible to critics who seek the key to his operations only in their metropolitan manifestations.

20. Dombey's obliviousness to gender as a distinct factor is already apparent in his assumption that Polly Toodles' maternal breast can be bought and replaced on the same principles as any other merchandise.

21. For example, Zwinger writes, "A daughter is anomalous in the patriarchal nuclear family. Virtually every other daughter in the canon occupies a place Dickens fudged for her by literally or figuratively removing her mother . . . or by de-sexualizing the father figure. . . . In either case the sexuality inherent in her separate desirable qualities is repressed beneath the sanctity and asexuality of the maternal role. . . . In *Dombey and Son* Dickens comes as close as he ever does to revealing the hollowness of his fictional, and his culture's ideological, daughter alibis" (1985:429–31).

22. This pattern is duplicated in the story of the Blimbers, the family responsible for Paul's fatally harsh schooling. Dr. Blimber educates his daughter, the short-haired and spectacled Cornelia, as an asexual duplicate of himself, then marries her to his assistant, Mr. Feeder, who will inherit the family business. The wistful and maternal Mrs. Blimber is the disposable factor in this successful family romance.

23. The Whittington figure reappears in *The Newcomes* (1:15) but as the long-dead founder of the banking dynasty. Unlike *Dombey and Son*, *The Newcomes* ends with the Colonel an actual penitent, a charity pensioner at his old school. The same fate—"refuge in one of them gent-eel almshouses of the better kind" (925)—is actually suggested for Dombey by one of his servants.

24. The main offices of the East India Company were located in Leadenhall Street until the Company's dissolution in 1858, when the center of imperial power shifted to the India office at Whitehall.

25. See Yelin's description of Dickens' change of mind about Edith's seduction and revenge, 1979:310–11.

26. See, for example, Welsh's discussion of Florence and Death, 1986:185–91.

27. See also "The Convict's Return" in *Pickwick Papers* and the many transportations and migrations in *David Copperfield*. Nineteenth-century representations of transportation and migration are discussed in more general terms by Brantlinger 1988:109–33.

28. Exile, migration, and transportation are the only alternatives (apart from death) Dickens allows the "fallen" woman. His interest in a project for reclaiming homeless women from the streets and outfitting them for migration as servants (with a view to finding honest husbands) is outlined in an article in *Household Words,* "Home for Homeless Women" (1913b:2:348–64).

Chapter 4. *"Fit Only for a Seraglio": The Discourse of Oriental Misogyny in* Jane Eyre *and* Vanity Fair

1. See also Wollstonecraft 1982:80 and 112. For "the true Mahometan strain" of Milton's Eve, see 1982:100.

2. I use the term *oriental misogyny* to indicate sensationalized Western representations of women's conditions in what was demarcated as "the Orient." These representations focused mainly on a range of practices like sati, polygamy, and parda that positioned "oriental" women as passive victims and their male masters as cruel and tyrannical, as against the more enlightened *idea* of gender relations supposedly existing in the West.

3. This chapter was, in fact, completed before the appearance of Meyer's essay. Although Meyer and I seem to cite several of the same passages, the conclusions we draw from them are somewhat different. Meyer comments in reference to Spivak's essay: "I find in *Jane Eyre* not Spivak's 'unquestioned ideology' of imperialism, but an ideology of imperialism which is questioned—and then reaffirmed—in interesting and illuminating ways" (1989:251–52). Although Meyer's article contains several interesting insights, especially about Brontë's juvenilia, I would dispute this conclusion and also her suggestion that the references to missionary activity in India at the end of *Jane Eyre* indicate an awareness of the problematic nature of empire.

4. Just as, Kaplan points out, Jane's declassed position as a governess "allowed the crisis of middle class femininity to be mapped on to the structural sexual vulnerability of all working-class servants" (1985:169).

5. "The notion of 'wildness' (or in its Latinate form 'savagery') belongs to a set of culturally self-authenticating devices which . . . includes the ideas of 'madness' and 'heresy' as well. These terms are used not merely to designate a specific condition . . . but also to confirm the value of their dialectical antithesis: 'civilization,' 'sanity,' and 'orthodoxy' respectively. Thus they . . . dictate a particular attitude governing a relationship between a lived reality and some area of problematical existence" (White 1972:4). Bertha's "madness" is integrally connected with her wildness and savagery, as well as with her female status.

6. See Gilbert and Gubar's discussion of Helen Burns, 1979:346.

7. Compare DuPlessis' account of Jean Rhys's fictional project in *Wide Sargasso Sea:* "By a maneuver of encirclement (entering the story before) and leverage (prying the story open), Rhys ruptures *Jane Eyre*. She returns us to a framework far from the triumphant individualism of the character Jane Eyre by concentrating on the colonial situation. . . . *Wide Sargasso Sea* states that the closures and precisions of any tale are purchased at the expense of the muted, even unspoken narrative, which writing beyond the ending will release" (1985:46).

8. Liddle and Joshi propose that British legislation sometimes worked for women (as in the abolition of sati) and sometimes against them (as in the removal of the matriarchal system in Kerala). They outline how British rule ignored the customary differences between caste and regional practices, for example, by codifying Brahmin texts as the sole authority on Hindu laws, thus imposing them on lower-caste women who had been subject to fewer customary restraints on their sexual freedom to divorce or remarry (1989:26–29).

9. "The use of an anglicised expression, Suttee, to denote a Hindu rite itself serves to illustrate a linguistic feature of the Indo-Western encounter. This feature has two aspects: one, the popular use of Western or anglicised Indian terms to describe Hindu rites and customs, and two, the often incorrect use of these terms" (Sharma 1976:590; see also Spivak 1985a).

The *OED* records the first English use of *suttee* in the Parliamentary Papers of 1786 and defines the word as "a Hindu widow who immolates herself on the funeral pile of her husband" and "the immolation of a Hindu Widow in this way." "Suttee" had entered into popular English usage by the first years of the nineteenth century.

Throughout this chapter I use the forms *sati* and *parda* rather than the anglicized terms, *suttee* and *purdah.*

10. Female emigration, the option in store for the independent-minded Rose Yorke in *Shirley,* and also adopted by Brontë's friend, Mary Taylor, was becoming an increasingly popular recourse for educated single women like Jane, as the formation of the Female Middle Class Emigration Society in 1862 suggests.

11. The implicit application is unmistakable in Lucy's stringent characterizations of her students: "Imprimis—it was clear that this swinish multitude were not to be driven by force. They were to be humoured, borne with very patiently: a courteous or sedate manner impressed them. . . . Severe or continuous mental application they could not, or would not bear. . . . They would riot for three additional lines to a lesson; but I never knew them to rebel against a wound given to their self-respect: the little they had of that quality was trained to be crushed, and it rather liked the pressure of a firm heel, than otherwise" (146–47).

12. See Hulme 1981 for a brilliant analysis of how the West Indian environment, in particular, was adapted into a discourse of empire through

seventeenth-century England's naturalization of words like *hurricane,* *Caribbean,* and *cannibal.*

13. According to Stein, the population of surplus women became a subject of public concern in the middle years of the century, after the appearance of Henry Mayhew's 1848 series on the large numbers of unattached *working* class women in London who were liable to be forced into prostitution (1978:266).

14. Thompson suggests that Tennyson's "Death of Oenone" is also "coloured by Anglo-Indian accounts of suttee" (1928:25).

15. Compare the letters of the English Eliza Fay, a Calcutta milliner in the early years of the nineteenth century. Fay, facing the personal and social consequences of a legal separation, writes home not of her own hardships but about the lives of Indian women: "And first for that horrible custom of widows burning themselves . . . I cannot suppose that the usage originated in the . . . ardent attachment of Indian wives towards their spouses. . . . I apprehend that . . . this practice is only a political scheme intended to insure the care and good offices of wives to their husbands, who have not failed in most countries to invent a sufficient number of rules to render the weaker sex totally subservient to their authority" (1925:201–3).

16. Sati had been unknown in this part of India before, an anomaly that has been seen as indicating a connection between the anxieties and tensions produced by colonization and increased violence toward women. Nandy suggests that it was the semi-Westernized "babu" class of Bengal that made "a sadistic sport out of sati. And to the extent this culture was itself a product of Western and modern encroachments upon the traditional lifestyle, sati was the society's weirdest response to new cultural inputs" (1975:178). Nandy links this expression of the culture's deepest misogyny to the increased worship of Kali in the early nineteenth century, suggesting that it was "as if some crucial sectors of Bengali society had lost all faith in the sustaining feminine principle in the environment and, in reaction, had built a more powerful symbol of womanly betrayal, punishment and rage" (1975:176).

17. See Mani's fascinating account of the British attempt to define and codify a "legal" sati through heavy-handed interpretations of inaccessible Hindu texts, 1985:107–27.

18. Coomaraswamy explores these religious and heroic models for theorizing sati in his 1924 essay on Indian women, drawing parallels between sati and the deaths of mythic European heroines like Alcestis, Dierdre, Brunhilde, Sigurd, and Joan of Arc (1985:92–95).

19. In this connection, see Rajan's essay on the representation of sati. Traditions of representation, Rajan argues, tend to glorify or eroticize sati and to ignore or elide its primary aspect of *pain.* Rajan suggests that "the condition of pain can serve adequately to define the human subject in certain contexts" (1990:6), thus enabling the construction in discourse of

the woman as a subject rather than a passive object or victim in the act of sati.

20. For a discussion of Thackeray's "calm, self-assured, uninformed British attitudes" to empire as revealed in his letters and essays, see Bearce 1961:242–50.

21. Interestingly, Bradden's enormously successful *Lady Audley's Secret* (1862) features a seemingly angelic but secretly murderous heroine who resorts to actual arson to preserve her hard-won social stability and who is finally committed to an asylum as at least latently insane.

22. Thackeray's novel was first published in monthly installments from January 1847 to July 1848. The first edition of *Jane Eyre* appeared in October 1847; the second, with its dedication to Thackeray, in December of the same year. Q. D. Leavis observes in her notes to the Penguin edition of *Jane Eyre:* "The Charades acted by the aristocratic party at Mr Rochester's house could not . . . have been imitated from the similar ones in *Vanity Fair* . . . though the converse is very possible" (485).

23. See also Ahmed's 1982 essay on Western perceptions of the harem, which focuses on European anxieties about the harem as a site of dangerous female autonomy and probable lesbian activity.

24. See also Alloula's *The Colonial Harem* (1986), which documents French attempts to invade the seclusion of the harem through compulsive reproductions of Algerian women in the public and degrading medium of the soft-porn picture postcard, and Barbara Harlow's introduction to the same work. However, I find Alloula's reproduction of these postcards in the gesture of "return[ing] this immense postcard to its sender"(5) somewhat troublesome because of his exclusion of the Algerian woman from this male transaction.

25. Sypher 1969 describes a 1775 farce, Irish playwright Isaac Bickerstaff's *The Sultan,* that is an intersting variation of this theme of male infiltration: It is the story of an English feminist Roxalana who enters and then attempts to reform the harem, a plot that immediately recalls Jane's provocative warning to Rochester (298).

26. On other textual and thematic connections between *Vanity Fair* and *Notes on a Journey,* see Musselwhite 1987:125–30.

27. See Fryer 1984:12–13 for the origins of the term *Hottentot,* a derogatory name for the Khoi-khoin peoples living around the Cape of Good Hope. *Hottentot* is already a byword of savagery in Johnson's *Rasselas,* though one Johnson himself challenges.

For the historical details on Saartjie (or Sarah) Bartmaan, her exhibition in London and Paris, and her death in France (where Cuvier's casts of her genitals and brain "may still be seen in the arrestingly named Musée de l'Homme"), see Fryer 1984:229–30. For representations of the "Hottentot Venus" in popular and commercial art and scientific texts, and for a more general discussion of the black female figure in European medical and aesthetic discourses, see Gilman 1985:204–42.

28. For a description of Matilda, a schoolgirl in Brontë's *Emma* whose original unattractiveness is cumulatively and indirectly identified as racial difference, see Meyer 1989:6.

29. See Musselwhite 1978:125 for a somewhat different reading of the Clytemnestra charade, in which he argues that the "collapse of Agamemnon into a riddle is facilitated by an Oriental setting."

Chapter 5. *"All the Girls Say Serve Him Right"*: The Multiple Anxieties of Edwin Drood

1. Enfantin, a Saint-Simonian, arrived in Egypt in the 1830s on a French intellectual and scientific expedition with a "mystic mission . . . to marry the mysterious 'mother' in the Orient" (quoted Bernal 1987:268–69). The canal itself was completed in the 1860s.

2. Arthur Cox annotates this in the Penguin edition of *Edwin Drood:* "At the opening of the second pyramid at Gizeh, the 6'6" Giovanni Batista Belzoni (1778–1823) became lodged in one of the tiny passages leading down into the burial chamber and was extricated with great difficulty" (304). Dickens seems to suggest a parallel between this orientalist's (incomplete) penetration of Egyptian tombs and Jasper's later probings in the crypts of Cloisterham. (The connection with Edwin's activities is made directly by Rosa.) We could also speculate about the link between the "half-choked" Belzoni and the strangulation (perhaps by "thuggee") that was to occur at the end of *Edwin Drood*.

3. Dickens' "Notes and Number Plans" are quoted at the end of the Penguin edition, 1986:286.

4. Even as Edwin accepts Rosa's termination of their engagement and begins to examine his own responsibility for its failure, he considers a similar relationship with Helena, based on the same sexual bravado and assurance of his own superiority: "It is with some misgivings of his own unworthiness that he thinks of her [Rosa], and of what they might have been to one another, if he had been more in earnest some time ago; if he had set a higher value on her. . . . And still, for all this, and though there is a sharp heartache in all this, the vanity and caprice of youth sustain that handsome figure of Miss Landless in the background of his mind" (176).

5. A similar but less comprehensive passage in *Great Expectations* links St. Paul's Cathedral with the slaughter houses of Smithfield and the prisons and transportations of Newgate.

6. For the Victorian debate over the morality of the opium wars, see Semmel 1970:152–54. Although the Tory opposition opposed the first opium war, liberal and radical opinion, including Exeter Hall and "reformers" like Macaulay and J. C. Hobhouse, firmly supported both the war and England's traffic in opium.

7. Trevelyan's is among the earliest voices heard against British drug trafficking. Berridge records that significant opposition did not begin until the establishment of the Society for the Suppression of the Opium

Trade in 1874. Not until the first decade of the twentieth century was the House of Commons able to agree that the opium trade was "morally indefensible" (1978:11–12). The traffic was finally suppressed in 1911.

8. For example, Kiernan cites an instance from W. H. Kingston's *Three Midshipmen* (1873) in which "opium was bad, to be sure, but so were the Chinese, who had broken a treaty, and if this went unpunished Britain would be leaving them 'to sink into the extreme of barbarism, towards which they appear to be hastening' " (1986:155).

For Dickens' own stinging comments on the Chinese, see his essay "The Chinese Junk" in *Miscellaneous Papers*, 1913:1:37–41.

9. De Quincey first visited Grasmere, the setting for many of William Wordsworth's best poems and of Dorothy Wordsworth's *Grasmere Journals*, in 1807, introduced by Coleridge, another literary opium voyager. De Quincey moved into Dove Cottage in 1809, after it grew too small for the expanding Wordsworth family, and remained its tenant until 1834.

10. De Quincey's gloss of "run amuck" directs the reader to "see the common accounts in any Eastern traveller or voyager of the frantic excesses committed by Malays who have taken opium or are reduced to desperation . . . by gambling" (92).

11. Sedgwick concludes that "the most exploratory of Victorians drew the borders of male homosexual culture to include exclusively, and almost exhaustively, the Mediterranean and the economically exploitable Third World" (1985:183).

12. The words *thug* and *thuggee* are used in quotation marks throughout this chapter to refer to a certain Victorian representation of Indian practices.

13. The plot of *The Moonstone* (first published in 1868 in Dickens' *All the Year Round*) also hinges on the effects of opium, and provides the direct link, if one is needed, between *Edwin Drood* and De Quincey's text. Collins' characters use "the far-famed *Confessions of an English Opium-Eater*" as evidence of "the capacity of a man to occupy himself actively, and to move about from place to place under the influence of opium" (1986:369–70).

14. Unsurprisingly, De Quincey's text suggests a similar configuration of opium, "thuggee," and menacing femininity in a description of one of his country expeditions: "There are, as perhaps the reader knows by experience, no jaguars in Wales . . . nor (generally speaking) any Thugs. What I feared most . . . was . . . some one of the many Brahminical-looking cows on the Cambrian hills . . . everywhere I observe in the feminine mind something of . . . that charming wilfulness which characterises our dear human sisters I fear through all worlds" (187).

15. The *OED* lists *jade* to mean, among other things, a "reprehensible woman or girl." *Jasper* is defined as "red, yellow or brown opaque quartze."

16. The Eyre case resulted in the execution of almost five hundred Jamaicans, including their leader, the Baptist preacher George William

Gordon, while many others were flogged, imprisoned, and tortured after trials of dubious legality. The case caused much public disagreement within the Victorian intelligentsia. The literary establishment (including Dickens, Carlyle, Tennyson, Kingsley, and Ruskin) lined up in favor of Eyre and "strong rule" in the colonies; Mill, Darwin, and lesser literary figures saw human rights as indivisible on grounds of race and formed the Jamaica Committee to seek Eyre's indictment. For a detailed account of the Eyre case, see Semmel 1969.

17. John Bright's "position in English politics was not too unlike that of George Gordon in the politics of Jamaica." He was regarded as "a red republican, a dangerous demagogue who did not hesitate to endanger the lives and property of the 'respectable classes' . . . by stirring up class antagonism. During the sixties Bright was to become the most hated and feared man in the country" (Semmel 1969:58). Bright also appears as the parliamentary bully Turnbull in Trollope's *Phineas Finn* (1869).

Richard Cobden was closely associated with Bright in his support for free trade and other "radical" causes. His most recent publication at the time of *Edwin Drood's* composition was probably the antimilitarist pamphlet on England's "annexation" of Burma, titled "How Wars are got up in India" (1867).

18. See Mill's discussion of the case in his *Autobiography:* "There was much more at stake than only justice to the Negroes, imperative as was that consideration. The question was, whether the British dependencies, and eventually perhaps Great Britain itself, were to be under the government of law or of military license; whether the lives and persons of British subjects are at the mercy of any two or three officers . . . whom a panic-stricken Governor or other functionary may assume the right to constitute into a so-called Court-Martial" (1969:175).

19. Berridge notes that the 1880s were marked by hostility to increased Chinese immigration, fear that opium consumption would spread to the Victorian middle classes, and a growing sense of the degeneracy and moral contamination of England (1978:15).

20. The argument for Jasper's involvement in "thuggee" has been made by several critics. Its main features are reviewed in Wilson's summary: "The thugs . . . had to commit their crimes with a fold of cloth which was a fragment of the gown of Kali. . . . This cloth had to be worn as Jasper's [black] scarf is. A secret burial place had to be selected, as Jasper selects Mrs Sapsea's tomb, before the murder took place. . . . The thug preys exclusively on travellers: Edwin Drood is going on a journey; and when Jasper, in his second opium dream . . . [discusses] . . . the murder, it is all in terms of a journey and a fellow-traveller. The Thug is to use exaggerated words of endearment. . . . Since Jasper is eventually caught, he is . . . to have slipped up in the ritual . . . he has overlooked the Thug superstition . . . that nothing but evil could come of murdering a man with any gold in his possession. Now Drood . . . is carrying the gold

ring . . . for Rosa; and we have it on Dickens' own testimony to Forster that the body is to be identified by this ring" (1941:87–89).

21. Critics have cited Helena's practice of disguising herself as a boy during frequent attempts to escape their cruel stepfather, her instant defiance of Jasper, and her determination to clear Neville of suspicion for the murder as support for the theory that she may be masquerading as Datchery.

22. Forster's biography assures Dickens' reader that "Rosa was to marry Tartar, and Crisparkle the sister of Landless, who was himself, I think, to have perished in assisting Tartar finally to unmask and seize the murderer" (quoted, "Introduction," *Edwin Drood*, 17).

Conclusion

1. See Said's far-reaching analysis in "Figures, Configurations, Transfigurations" (1990) for a related discussion of Lewis' editorial.

References

Abrahams, Roger D. and John F. Szwed, eds. 1983. *After Africa*. New Haven: Yale University Press.

Ahmed, Leila. 1982. "Western Ethnocentrism and Perceptions of the Harem." *Feminist Studies* (Fall), 8(3):521–34.

Alexander, Michael and Sushila Anand. 1980. *Queen Victoria's Maharajah*. London: Weidenfeld and Nicholson.

Alloula, Malek. 1986. *The Colonial Harem*. Trans. Myrna Godzich and Wlad Godzich. Minneapolis: University of Minnesota Press.

Althusser, Louis. 1971. *Lenin and Philosophy and Other Essays*. Trans. Ben Brewster. New York: Monthly Review Press.

Anderson, Benedict. 1990. "Murder and Progress in Modern Siam." *New Left Review* (May-June), 181:33–48.

Andrews, K. R. et al., eds. 1979. *The Westward Enterprise: English Activities in Ireland, the Atlantic, and America 1480–1650*. Detroit: Wayne State University Press.

Arendt, Hannah. 1968. *Imperialism*. New York: Harcourt Brace Jovanovich.

Armstrong, Nancy. 1987. *Desire and Domestic Fiction*. New York: Oxford University Press.

Atkinson, Colin B. and Jo Atkinson. 1984. "Maria Edgeworth, *Belinda*, and Women's Rights." *Eire-Ireland* (Winter), 19(4):94–118.

Auerbach, Nina. 1981. "Jane Austen and Romantic Imprisonment." In Monaghan 1981:9–27.

———1985. *Romantic Imprisonment.* New York: Columbia University Press.

———1987. "Engorging the Patriarchy." In Benstock 1987:150–60.

Austen, Jane. 1952. *Letters to her Sister Cassandra and Others.* R. W. Chapman, ed. London: Oxford University Press.

———1984. *Persuasion.* Harmondsworth: Penguin.

———1984. *Lady Susan/The Watsons/Sanditon.* 1984. Harmondsworth: Penguin.

———1985. *Mansfield Park.* Harmondsworth: Penguin.

———1985. *Emma.* Harmondsworth: Penguin.

———1985. *Northanger Abbey.* Harmondsworth: Penguin.

Banfield, Ann. 1981. "The Influence of Place: Jane Austen and the Novel of Social Consciousness." In Monaghan 1981:28–47.

Barbauld, Anna Laetitia. 1825. *Works.* London: Longman, Hurst, Rees and Co.

Barker, Francis et al., eds. 1978. *1848: The Sociology of Literature.* Essex Conference on the Sociology of Literature. Colchester: University of Essex.

———1981. *1642: Literature and Power in the Seventeenth Century.* Colchester: University of Essex,

———1985. *Europe and Its Others.* 2 vols. Essex Conference on the Sociology of Literature. Colchester: University of Essex.

———1986. *Literature, Politics and Theory.* London: Methuen.

Barthelemy, Anthony Gerard. 1987. *Black Face Maligned Race.* Baton Rouge: Louisiana State University Press.

Baudet, Henri. 1965. *Paradise on Earth: Some Thoughts on European Images of Non-European Man.* New Haven: Yale University Press.

Bearce, George D. 1961. *British Attitudes Towards India 1784–1858.* London: Oxford University Press.

Beer, Gillian. 1978. "Carlyle and *Mary Barton:* Problems of Utterance." In Barker 1978:242–55.

Benstock, Shari, ed. 1987. *Feminist Issues in Literary Scholarship.* Bloomington: Indiana University Press.

Berger, John. 1972. *Ways of Seeing.* London: BBC.

Bernal, Martin. 1987. *Black Athena,* vol. 1: *The Fabrication of Ancient Greece 1785–1985.* New Brunswick: Rutgers University Press.

Berridge, Virginia. 1978. "East End Opium Dens and Narcotic Use in Britain." *The London Journal* 4(1):3–28.

Bhabha, Homi K. 1984. "Representation and the Colonial Text: A Critical Exploration of Some Forms of Mimeticism." In Frank Gloversmith, ed., *The Theory of Reading,* 93–122. Sussex: Harvester Press.

———1985. "Signs Taken for Wonders: Questions of Ambivalence and Authority under a Tree Outside Delhi, May 1817." *Critical Inquiry* (Autumn), 12(1):144–65.

——1986. "The Other Question: Difference, Discrimination and the Discourse of Colonialism." In Barker 1986:148–72.

Bilby, Kenneth and Filomina Steady. 1981. "Black Women and Survival: A Maroon Case." In Filomina Steady, ed., *The Black Woman Cross-Culturally*, 451–67. Cambridge, Mass.: Schenkman.

Bodelson, C. A. 1960. *Studies in Mid-Victorian Imperialism*. London: Heinemann.

Bolt, Christine. 1971. *Victorian Attitudes to Race*. London: Routledge, Kegan Paul.

Boswell, James. 1953. *Life of Johnson*. Oxford: Oxford University Press.

Brantlinger, Patrick. 1985. "Victorians and Africans: The Genealogy of the Myth of the Dark Continent." *Critical Inquiry* (Autumn), 12(1):166–203.

——1988. *Rule of Darkness*. Ithaca: Cornell University Press.

Brontë, Charlotte. 1974. *Jane Eyre*. Harmondsworth: Penguin.

Brunton, Mary. 1986. *Discipline*. London: Pandora Press.

Bulwer-Lytton, Edward George. 1849. *The Caxtons*. Boston: Little, Brown.

Butler, Marilyn. 1972. *Maria Edgeworth: A Literary Biography*. Oxford: Oxford University Press.

——1982. *Romantics, Rebels and Reactionaries*. Oxford: Oxford University Press.

Carlyle, Thomas. 1849. "Occasional Discourses on the Negro Question." *Fraser's Magazine* (December), 671–79.

——1883. *Chartism: Miscellaneous Essays*, vol. 3. London: Chapman and Hall, 1883.

Carter, Paul. 1988. *The Road to Botany Bay*. New York: Alfred A. Knopf.

Cell, John. 1979. "The Imperial Conscience." In Peter Marsh, ed., *The Conscience of the Victorian State*, 173–213. Syracuse: Syracuse University Press.

Christian, Barbara. 1988. "The Race for Theory." *Feminist Studies* (Spring), 14(1):67–79.

Clark, Robert. 1984. "Riddling the Family Firm: The Sexual Economy in *Dombey and Son*." *ELH* (Spring), 51(1):69–84.

Clarke, Isabel C. 1949. *Maria Edgeworth: Her Family and Friends*. London: Hutchinson.

Cobbett, William. 1804. *Cobbett's Weekly Political Register*, June 16, 1804, 24.

——1985. *Rural Rides*. Harmondsworth: Penguin.

Cohn, Bernard S. 1983. "Representing Authority in Victorian India." In Eric Hobsbawm and Terence Ranger, eds. *The Invention of Tradition*, 165–209. Cambridge: Cambridge University Press.

Collins, Wilkie. 1986. *The Moonstone*. New York: Bantam.

Colls, Robert and Philip Dodd, eds. 1986. *Englishness Politics and Culture 1880–1920*. London: Croom Helm.

Conant, Martha Pike. 1908. *The Oriental Tale in England in the Eighteenth Century.* New York: Columbia University Press.

Coomaraswamy, Ananda. 1985. "Status of Indian Women." *The Dance of Siva*, 82–102. New York: Dover.

Cooper, Anna Julia. 1988. *Slavery and the French Revolution (1788–1905).* Lewistown: Edwin Mellen Press.

Courtright, Paul B. 1988. "The Iconographies of *Sati*." "New Light on *Sati*/Suttee" Conference. Southern Asia Institute, Columbia University, October 21.

Craton, Michael. 1982. *Testing the Chains: Resistance to Slavery in the British West Indies.* Ithaca: Cornell University Press.

Crosby, Alfred. 1986. *Ecological Imperialism: The Biological Expansion of Europe, 900–1900.* Cambridge: Cambridge University Press.

Dabydeen, David, ed. 1985. *The Black Presence in English Literature.* Manchester: Manchester University Press.

——1987. *Hogarth's Blacks.* Athens: University of Georgia Press.

Dadzie, Stella. 1990. "Searching for the Invisible Woman: Slavery and Resistance in Jamaica." *Race and Class* (October-December), 32(2):21–38.

Daniell, David. 1985. "Buchan and the 'Black General.'" In Dabydeen 1985:135–67.

David, Deirdre. 1987. *Intellectual Women and Victorian Patriarchy.* London: Macmillan.

Davies, Phillips G. 1961. "The Miscegenation Theme in the Works of Thackeray." *MLN* (April), 76(4):326–31.

Davin, Anna. 1978. "Imperialism and Motherhood." *History Workshop,* 5:9–65.

Defoe, Daniel. 1823. *The Life, Adventures and Piracies of the Famous Captain Singleton.* London: J. M. Dent.

Deforest, Mary. 1987. "Mrs Elton and the Slave Trade." *Persuasions* (December 16), 9:11–13.

De Quincey, Thomas. 1971. *Confessions of an English Opium Eater.* Harmondsworth: Penguin.

DiBattista, Maria. 1980. "The Triumph of Clytemnestra." *PMLA* (October), 95(5):827–37.

Dickens, Charles. 1913a. "The Niger Expedition." *Miscellaneous Papers,* 1:45–67. London: MacDonald.

——1913b. "Home for Homeless Women." *Miscellaneous Papers,* 1:348–64. London: MacDonald.

——1970. *Dealings with the Firm of Dombey and Son: Wholesale, Retail and for Exportation.* Harmondsworth: Penguin.

——1977. *Bleak House.* New York: W. W. Norton.

——1986. *The Mystery of Edwin Drood.* Harmondsworth: Penguin.

Dickinson, G. Lowes. 1946. *Letters from John Chinaman and Other Essays.* London: Allen and Unwin.

Disraeli, Benjamin. 1984. *Sybil.* Harmondsworth: Penguin.

Dudley, Edward and Maximillian E. Novak, eds. 1972. *The Wild Man Within: An Image in Western Thought from the Renaissance to Romanticism.* Pittsburgh: University of Pittsburgh Press.

DuPlessis, Rachel Blau. 1985. *Writing Beyond the Ending.* Bloomington: Indiana University Press.

Dykes, Eva Beatrice. 1942. *The Negro in English Romantic Thought.* Washington, D.C.: Associated Publishers.

Eagleton, Terry. 1975. *Myths of Power: A Marxist Study of the Brontës.* London: Macmillan.

——1978. *Criticism and Ideology.* London: Verso.

Edgeworth, Maria. 1986. *Belinda.* London: Pandora Press.

——1964. *Castle Rackrent.* Oxford: Oxford University Press.

——1969a. "The Grateful Negro." *Moral Tales.* Hildesheim: Georg Olsm Verlagsbuchhandlung.

——1969b. *The Absentee: Tales of Fashionable Life.* Hildesheim: Georg Olsm Verlagsbuchhandlung.

Edwards, Paul. 1985. "Black Writers of the Eighteenth and Nineteenth Centuries." In Dabydeen 1985:50–67.

Fabian, Johannes. 1983. *Time and the Other.* New York: Columbia University Press.

Fanon, Frantz. 1966. *The Wretched of the Earth.* Trans. Constance Farrington. New York: Grove Press.

——1967a. *Black Skin, White Masks.* Trans. Charles Markmann. New York: Grove Press.

——1967b. *A Dying Colonialism.* Trans. Haakon Chevalier. New York: Grove Press.

Fay, Eliza. 1925. *Original Letters from India.* London: Hogarth Press.

Ferguson, Moira, ed. 1987. *The History of Mary Prince, a West Indian Slave, Related by Herself.* London: Pandora Press.

Fielding, K. J. 1952. "*Edwin Drood* and Governor Eyre." *Listener* (December), 25:1083–84.

Figueira, Dorothy. 1988. "Die Flamberte Frau: Reflections on *Sati* in European Culture." "New Light on *Sati*/Suttee" Conference, Southern Asia Institute, Columbia University, October 21.

Foucault, Michel. 1976. *The Archaeology of Knowledge and the Discourse on Language.* New York: Harper and Row.

Foster, William. 1924. *The East India House.* London: Bodley Head.

Fox-Genovese, Elizabeth and Eugene D. Genovese. 1983. *Fruits of Merchant Capital.* New York: Oxford University Press.

Fryer, Peter. 1984. *Staying Power: The History of Black People in Britain.* London: Pluto Press.

Gallagher, Catherine. 1985. *The Industrial Reformation of English Fiction.* Chicago: Chicago University Press.

Gallop, Jane. 1988. *Thinking Through the Body.* New York: Columbia University Press.

Gaskell, Elizabeth. 1970a. *Mary Barton.* Harmondsworth: Penguin.

——1970b. *North and South.* Harmondsworth: Penguin.

Gilbert, Sandra M. and Susan Gubar. 1979. *The Madwoman in the Attic.* New Haven: Yale University Press.

Gilman, Sander L. 1985. "Black Bodies, White Bodies: Toward an Iconography of Female Sexuality in Late Nineteenth-Century Art, Medicine, and Literature." *Critical Inquiry* (Autumn), 12(1):204–242.

Goonatilake, Susantha. 1982. *Crippled Minds.* Colombo, Sri Lanka: Lake House.

Gooneratne, Yasmine. 1968. *English Literature in Ceylon 1815–1878.* Dehiwala, Sri Lanka: Tisara Prakasakayo.

Green, Martin. 1979. *Dreams of Adventure, Deeds of Empire.* New York: Basic Books.

Green, Michael. 1978. "Notes on Fathers and Sons from *Dombey and Son.*" In Barker 1978:256–64.

Greenburger, Alan J. 1967. *The British Image of India: The Literature of Imperialism, 1880–1960.* Oxford: Oxford University Press.

Guha, Ranajit, ed. 1982, 1983, 1984. *Subaltern Studies.* 3 vols. Delhi: Oxford University Press.

Hammond, Dorothy and Alta Jablow. 1974. *The Africa That Never Was.* New York: Twayne Publishers.

Hancock, LynNell. 1990. "Whose America Is This, Anyway?" *Village Voice,* April 24, 37–39.

Harden, Elizabeth. 1984. *Maria Edgeworth.* Boston: Twayne Publishers.

Hawthorne, Mark D. 1975. "Maria Edgeworth's Unpleasant Lesson: The Shaping of Character." *Studies* (Summer), 64(254):167–77.

Hecht, J. Jean. 1954. *Continental and Colonial Servants in Eighteenth Century England.* Northampton, Mass.: Smith.

Heilbrun Carolyn G. 1988. *Writing a Woman's Life.* New York: W. W. Norton.

Heilbrun, Carolyn G. and Margaret R. Higonnet, eds. 1983. *The Representation of Women in Fiction.* Baltimore: Johns Hopkins University Press.

Helly, Dorothy O. 1987. *Livingstone's Legacy.* Athens: Ohio University Press.

Hennelly, Mark M., Jr. 1985. "Detecting Collins' Diamond: From Serpentstone to Moonstone." *Nineteenth Century Fiction* (March), 39(1):25–47.

Hennessy, Rosemary and Rajeswari Mohan. 1989. "The Construction of Woman in Three Popular Texts of Empire: Towards a Critique of Materialist Feminism." *Textual Practice* (Winter), 3(3):323–59.

Hobsbawm, Eric. 1987. *The Age of Empire 1875–1914.* New York: Pantheon.

Hobson, J. A. 1965. *Imperialism.* Ann Arbor: University of Michigan Press.

hooks, bell. 1981. *Ain't I a Woman.* Boston: South End Press.

——1990. *Yearning: Race, Gender, and Cultural Politics.* Boston: South End Press.

Howe, Susanne. 1949. *Novels of Empire.* New York: Columbia University Press.

Hull, Gloria T., Patricia Bell Scott, and Barbara Smith, eds. 1982. *But Some of Us Are Brave*. Old Westbury, N.Y.: The Feminist Press.

Hulme, Peter. 1981. "Hurricanes in the Caribbees: The Constitution of the Discourse of English Colonialism." In Barker 1981:54–83.

———1985. "Balzac's Parisian Mystery: La Cousine Bette and the Writing of Historical Criticism." *Literature and History* (Spring), 11(1):47–64.

———1986. *Colonial Encounters*. London: Methuen.

Hunter, William. 1897. *The Thackerays in India*. Oxford: Oxford University Press.

Hurst, Michael. 1969. *Maria Edgeworth and the Public Scene*. Coral Gables, Fla.: Miami University Press.

Hutchins, Francis G. 1967. *The Illusion of Permanence*. Princeton: Princeton University Press.

James, C. L. R. 1963. *Black Jacobins*. New York: Alfred A. Knopf.

———1983. *Beyond a Boundary*. New York: Pantheon.

Jameson, Frederic. 1981. *The Political Unconscious*. Ithaca: Cornell University Press.

———1990. "Modernism and Imperialism." In Terry Eagleton, Frederic Jameson, and Edward Said. *Nationalism, Colonialism and Literature*, 43–66. Minneapolis: University of Minnesota Press.

JanMohamed, Abdul R. 1983. *Manichean Aesthetics*. Amherst: University of Massachusetts Press.

Johnson, Claudia L. 1989. "A 'Sweet Face as White as Death': Jane Austen and the Politics of Female Sensibility." *Novel* (Winter), 22(2):159–74.

Johnson, Edgar. 1979. *Charles Dickens: His Tragedy and Triumph*. Harmondsworth: Penguin.

Johnson, Lemuel A. 1969. *The Devil, the Gargoyle, and the Buffoon: The Negro as Metaphor in Western Literature*. Port Washington, N.Y.: Kennikat Press.

Jordan, Winthrop D. 1968. *White Over Black*. Chapel Hill: University of North Carolina Press.

Kaplan, Cora. 1985. "Pandora's Box: Subjectivity, Class and Sexuality in Socialist Feminist Criticism." In Gayle Greene and Coppelia Kahn, eds., *Making a Difference*, 146–76. London: Methuen.

Kelly, Gary. 1989. *English Fiction of the Romantic Period 1789–1830*. London: Longman.

Kenny, Virginia C. 1984. *The Country-House Ethos in English Literature 1688–1750*. Sussex: Harvester Press.

Kiernan V. G. 1982. "Tennyson, King Arthur and Imperialism." In Raphael Samuel and Gareth Stedman Jones, eds., *Culture, Ideology and Politics*, 126–148. London: Routledge, Kegan Paul.

———1986. *Lords of Humankind*. New York: Columbia University Press.

Kingsley, Charles. 1983. *Alton Locke*. Oxford: Oxford University Press.

Kirkham, Margaret. 1983. *Jane Austen, Feminism, and Fiction*. Totowa, N.J.: Barnes and Noble.

Kucich, John. 1989. "Clearing a Path." *Novel* (Winter), 22(2):216–18.

Le Breton, Anna. 1874. *Memoir of Mrs Barbauld.* London: George Bell and Sons.

Lewis, Bernard. 1988. "'Western Culture Must Go.'" *The Wall Street Journal,* May 2, 24.

Liddle, Joanna and Rama Joshi. 1989. *Daughters of Independence: Gender, Caste and Class in India.* New Brunswick: Rutgers University Press.

Lorimer, Douglas A. 1978. *Colour, Class and the Victorians.* Leicester: Leicester University Press.

Lukacs, Georg. 1962. *The Historical Novel.* Trans. Hannah and Stanley Mitchell. London: Merlin.

McClure, John A. 1981. *Kipling and Conrad: The Colonial Fiction.* Cambridge: Harvard University Press.

Macherey, Pierre. 1978. *A Theory of Literary Production.* Trans. Geoffrey Wall. London: Routledge, Kegan Paul.

Mackenzie, John M., ed. 1986. *Imperialism and Popular Culture.* Manchester: Manchester University Press.

Magdoff, Harry. 1978. *Imperialism.* New York: Monthly Review Press.

Mani, Lata. 1985. "The Production of an Official Discourse on *Sati* in Early Nineteenth Century Bengal." In Barker 1985:1:107–27.

Marcus, Jane. 1983. "Liberty, Sorority, Misogyny." In Heilbrun and Higonnet 1983:60–97.

——1987. "Still Practice, A/Wrested Alphabet: Toward a Feminist Aesthetic." In Benstock 1987:79–97.

Martineau Harriet. 1833. "Cinnamon and Pearls: A Tale." *Illustrations of Political Economy,* vol. 7. London: Charles Fox.

——1857. *The History of British Rule in India.* London: Smith Elder.

——1969. *Retrospect of Western Travel.* 2 vols. New York: Greenwood Press.

Marx, Karl. 1977. *The Eighteenth Brumaire of Louis Bonaparte.* New York: International Publishers.

——1981. *Capital.* New York: Vintage, 1981.

Maughan-Brown, David. 1985. *Land, Freedom and Fiction.* London: Zed Books.

Mazlish, Bruce. 1973. *James and John Stuart Mill.* New York: Basic Books.

Mazumdar, Vina. 1978. "Comment on Suttee." *Signs* (Winter), 4(2):269–73.

Memmi, Albert. 1967. *The Colonizer and the Colonized.* Boston: Beacon Press.

Meredith, George. 1968. *The Egoist.* Harmondsworth: Penguin.

Meyer, Susan. 1989. "Colonialism and the Figurative Strategies of *Jane Eyre.*" *Victorian Studies* (Winter), 33(2):247–68.

Mill, James. 1969. *On Education.* W. H. Burston, ed. Cambridge: Cambridge University Press.

Mill, John Stuart. 1850. "The Negro Question." *Fraser's Magazine* (January), 25–31.

——1969. *Autobiography.* Boston: Houghton Mifflin.

Mitchell, W. J. T., ed. 1983. *The Politics of Interpretation*. Chicago: University of Chicago Press.

Mitter, Partha. 1977. *Much Maligned Monsters*. Oxford: Clarendon Press.

Miyoshi, Masao. 1969. *The Divided Self*. New York: New York University Press.

Mohanty, Chandra. 1988. "Under Western Eyes: Feminist Scholarship and Colonial Discourse." *Feminist Review* (Autumn), 30:61–88.

Monaghan, David, ed. 1981. *Jane Austen in a Social Context*. Totowa, N.J.: Barnes and Noble.

Moynahan, Julian. 1962. "Dealings with the Firm of Dombey and Son: Firmness Versus Wetness." In John Gross and Gabriel Pearson, eds., *Dickens and the Twentieth Century*, 121–31. Toronto: University of Toronto Press.

Mukherjee, Ramkrishna. 1974. *The Rise and Fall of the East India Company*. New York: Monthly Review Press.

Musselwhite, David. E. 1978. "The Novel as Narcotic." In Barker 1978:207–24.

——1986. "The Trial of Warren Hastings." In Barker 1986:77–103.

——1987. *Partings Welded Together: Politics and Desire in the Nineteenth Century Novel*. London: Methuen.

Nandy, Ashis. 1975. "Sati: A Nineteenth Century Tale of Women, Violence and Protest." In V. C. Joshi, ed., *Rammohun Roy and the Process of Modernization in India*, 168–94. Delhi: Vikas.

——1983. *The Intimate Enemy Loss and Recovery of Self Under Colonialism*. New Delhi: Oxford University Press.

Nerlich, Michael. 1987. *The Ideology of Adventure*, vol. 1. Trans. Ruth Crowley. Minneapolis: University of Minnesota Press.

Newton, Judith. 1987. "Making—and Remaking—History: Another Look at 'Patriarchy.'" In Benstock 1987:124–40.

Newton, Judith and Deborah Rosenfelt, eds. 1985. *Feminist Criticism and Social Change*. New York: Methuen.

Ngugi, Wa Thiong'o. 1986. *Decolonising the Mind*. London: James Currey.

Oddie, William. 1972. "Dickens and the Indian Mutiny." *The Dickensian* (January), 68(1):3–15.

Owenson, Sydney (Lady Morgan). 1986. *The Wild Irish Girl*. London: Pandora Press.

Panikkar, K. M. 1959. *Asia and Western Dominance*. London: Allen and Unwin.

Parks, Fanny. 1850. *Wanderings of a Pilgrim in Search of the Picturesque, During Four-and-Twenty Years in the East; with Revelations of Life in the Zenana*. 2 vols. London: Pelham Richardson.

Parry, Benita. 1987. "Problems in Current Theories of Colonial Discourse." *Oxford Literary Review* 9(1–2):27–57.

Politi, Jina. 1982. "*Jane Eyre* Class-ified." *Literature and History* (Spring), 8(1):56–66.

Poovey, Mary. 1984. *The Proper Lady and the Woman Writer.* Chicago: University of Chicago Press.

——1988. *Uneven Developments.* Chicago: University of Chicago Press.

Purchas, Samuel. 1613. *Purchas His Pilgrimage.* London: H. Featherstone.

Ragatz, Lowell J. 1928. *The Fall of the Planter Class in the British Caribbean.* New York: Century.

Rajan, Rajeswari Sunder. 1990. "The Subject of Sati: Pain and Death in the Contemporary Discourse on Sati." *Yale Journal of Criticism* 3(2):1–27.

Ranger, Terence. 1983. "The Invention of Tradition." In Eric Hobsbawm and Terence Ranger, eds., *The Invention of Tradition,* 211–62. Cambridge: Cambridge University Press.

Raskin, Jonah. 1971. *The Mythology of Imperialism.* New York: Random House.

Ray, Gordon N. 1955. *Thackeray: The Uses of Adversity.* New York: McGraw-Hill.

Reed, John R. 1973. "English Imperialism and the Unacknowledged Crime of *The Moonstone.*" *Clio* (June), 2(3):281–90.

Rich, Adrienne. 1979. "*Jane Eyre:* The Temptations of a Motherless Woman." *On Lies, Secrets and Silence,* 88–106. New York: W. W. Norton.

Richon, Olivier. 1985. "Representation, the Despot and the Harem: Some Questions around an Academic Orientalist Painting by Lecomte-du-Nouy." In Barker 1985:1:1–13.

Ritvo, Harriet. 1987. *The Animal Estate The English and Other Creatures in the Victorian Age.* Cambridge: Harvard University Press.

Robinson, Ronald, John Gallagher, and Alice Denny. 1961. *Africa and the Victorians.* New York: St. Martin's Press.

Rose, Phyllis. 1984. *Parallel Lives.* New York: Vintage.

Said, Edward W. 1979. *Orientalism.* New York: Vintage.

——1983. *The World, the Text, and the Critic.* Cambridge: Harvard University Press.

——1986. "Orientalism Reconsidered." In Barker 1986:210–29.

——1989. "Jane Austen and Empire." In Terry Eagleton, ed., *Raymond Williams: Critical Perspectives,* 150–64. Boston: Northeastern University Press.

——1990. "Figures, Configurations, Transfigurations." *Race and Class* (July-September), 32(1):1–16.

Sandison, Alan. 1967. *The Wheel of Empire.* New York: St. Martin's Press.

Sangari, Kumkum and Sudesh Vaid, eds. 1989. *Recasting Women.* New Brunswick: Rutgers University Press.

Schaub, Uta Liebmann. 1989. "Foucault's Oriental Subtext." *PMLA* 4(3):306–16.

Schipper, Mineke, ed. 1985. *Unheard Words.* Trans. Barbara Potter Fasting. London: Allison and Busby.

Schreiner, Olive. 1978. *Woman and Labour*. London: Virago Press.

Scott, Joan Wallach. 1988. *Gender and the Politics of History*. New York: Columbia University Press.

Sedgwick, Eve. 1985. *Between Men*. New York: Columbia University Press.

Seeley, J. R. 1972. *The Expansion of England*. Chicago: Chicago University Press.

Semmel, Bernard. 1969. *Democracy Versus Empire*. New York: Anchor.

——1970. *The Rise of Free Trade Imperialism: Classical Political Economy, the Empire of Free Trade, and Imperialism*. Cambridge: Cambridge University Press.

Sharma, Arvind. 1976. "Suttee: A Study in Western Reactions." *Journal of Indian History* 54(3):589–612.

Showalter, Elaine. 1978. "Family Secrets and Domestic Subversion: Rebellion in the Novels of the 1860s." In Wohl 1978:101–16.

Sleeman, William. 1971. *Sleeman in Oudh*. P. D. Reeves, ed. Cambridge: Cambridge University Press.

Smith, Bernard. 1985. *European Vision and the South Pacific*. New Haven: Yale University Press.

Spear, Percival. 1965. *A History of India*. Harmondsworth: Penguin.

Spender, Dale, ed. 1983. *Feminist Theorists*. New York: Random House.

——1986. *Mothers of the Novel*. London: Pandora Press.

Spivak, Gayatri Chakravorty. 1985a. "Three Women's Texts and a Critique of Imperialism." *Critical Inquiry* (Autumn), 12(1):243–61.

——1985b. "Can the Subaltern Speak? Speculations on Widow-Sacrifice." *Wedge* (Winter/Spring), 7/8:120–30.

——1985c. "The Rani of Sirmur." In Barker 1985:1:128–51.

——1987. *In Other Worlds*. New York: Methuen.

——1990. *The Post-Colonial Critic*. Sarah Harasym, ed. New York: Routledge.

Staves, Susan. 1980/81. "British Seduced Maidens." *Eighteenth-Century Studies* 14(2):109–34.

Stein, Dorothy K. 1978. "Women to Burn: Suttee as a Normative Institution." *Signs* 4(2):253–68.

Stevenson, Robert Louis. 1983. *The Master of Ballantrae*. Oxford: Oxford University Press.

Stocking, George. 1987. *Victorian Anthropology*. New York: Free Press.

Stokes, Eric. 1959. *The English Utilitarians in India*. Oxford: Clarendon Press.

Street, Brian. 1979. *The Savage in Literature*. London: Routledge, Kegan Paul.

——1985. "Reading the Novels of Empire: Race and Ideology in the Classic 'Tale of Adventure.' " In Dabydeen 1985:95–111.

Summers, Anne. 1975. *Damned Whores and God's Police*. Ringwood, Victoria: Penguin.

Sutherland, John. 1970. "Thackeray as a Victorian Racialist." *Essays in Criticism* (October), 20(4):441–45.

Sypher, Wylie. 1939. "The West Indian as a 'Character' in the Eighteenth Century." *Studies in Philology* (July), 36(3):503–20.

——1969. *Guineas's Captive Kings*. New York: Octagon.

Temperley, Howard. 1972. *British Antislavery 1833–1870*. London: Longman.

Thackeray, William. 1868. *The Newcomes*. 2 vols. London: Smith, Elder.

——1869. *Notes of a Journey from Cornhill to Grand Cairo*. London: Smith, Elder.

——1964. *The Letters and Papers of William Makepeace Thackeray*. 3 vols. Gordon N. Ray, ed. Cambridge: Harvard University Press.

——1968. *Vanity Fair*. Harmondsworth: Penguin.

Thapar, Romila. 1973. *The Past and Prejudice*. New Delhi: Ministry of Information and Broadcasting.

Thompson, Edward. 1928. *Suttee*. London: Allen and Unwin.

Trevelyan, G. O. 1866. *Competition Wallah*. London: np.

Trinh, T. Minh-ha. 1989. *Woman, Native, Other*. Bloomington: Indiana University Press.

Turner, Bryan S. 1978. *Marx and the End of Orientalism*. London: Allen and Unwin.

Uglow, Jenny. 1983. "From Sympathy to Theory." In Spender 1983:146–62.

Vicinus, Martha, ed. 1977. *A Widening Sphere*. Bloomington: Indiana University Press.

Visram, Rozina. 1986. *Ayahs, Lascars, and Princes*. London: Pluto Press.

Viswanathan, Gauri. 1989. *Masks of Conquest: Literary Study and British Rule in India*. New York: Columbia University Press.

Waley, Arthur. 1968. *The Opium War Through Chinese Eyes*. Stanford: Stanford University Press.

Weissman, Judith. 1987. *Half Savage and Hardy and Free*. Middletown, Conn.: Wesleyan University Press.

Welsh, Alexander. 1986. *The City of Dickens*. Cambridge: Harvard University Press.

White, Hayden. 1972. "The Forms of Wildness: Archaeology of an Idea." In Dudley and Novak 1972:3–38.

Wikkramasinha, Lakdasa. 1976. "Don't talk to me about Matisse." *Journal of South Asian Literature* (Fall/Winter), 12(1 and 2):83.

Williams, Eric. 1944. *Capitalism and Slavery*. Chapel Hill: University of North Carolina Press.

——1970a. *From Columbus to Castro*. London: André Deutsch.

——1972. *British Historians and the West Indies*. New York: Americana Press.

Williams, Raymond. 1970b. Introduction. In Dickens 1970.

——1973. *The Country and the City*. New York: Oxford University Press.

—1981. *Politics and Letters.* London: Verso.

—1983a. *Culture and Society.* New York: Columbia University Press.

—1983b. *Keywords.* New York: Oxford University Press.

Wilson, Angus. 1986. Introduction. In Dickens 1986.

Wilson. Edmund. 1941. *The Wound and the Bow.* Boston: Houghton Mifflin.

Wohl, Anthony S., ed. 1978. *The Victorian Family.* London: Croom Helm.

Wollstonecraft, Mary. 1982. *A Vindication of the Rights of Woman.* Harmondsworth: Penguin.

Woolf, Leonard. 1961. *Growing.* London: Hogarth Press.

Woolf, Virginia. 1929. *A Room of One's Own.* San Diego: Harcourt Brace Jovanovich.

—1938. *Three Guineas.* San Diego: Harcourt Brace Jovanovich.

Wordsworth, William. 1971. *The Prelude.* J. C. Maxwell, ed. Harmondsworth: Penguin.

Wurgaft, Lewis D. 1983. *The Imperial Imagination.* Middletown, Conn.: Wesleyan University Press.

Yelin, Louise. 1979. "Strategies for Survival: Florence and Edith in *Dombey and Son.*" *Victorian Studies* (Spring), 22(3):297–319.

Zastoupil, Lynn. 1988. "J. S. Mill and India." *Victorian Studies* (Autumn), 32(1):31–54.

Zwinger, Lynda. 1985. "The Fear of the Father: Dombey and Daughter." *Nineteenth Century Fiction* (March), 39(4):420–40.

Index

Abolitionism, British, 12, 19, 22, 30
Adams, Brooks, 47
Addison, Joseph, 6, 37
Alloula, Malek, 141n24
Armstrong, Nancy, 40, 60
Atkinson, Colin B., 19–20
Atkinson, Jo, 19–20
Auerbach, Nina, 41, 64–65, 70, 83, 136n12
Austen, Jane, 21; *Emma*, 41–42, 81; *Mansfield Park*, 19, 42–45, 49, 57, 68; *Northanger Abbey*, 81; *Persuasion;* 13, 39–46, 49–51, 68; *Pride and Prejudice*, 13, 41; *Sanditon*, 43–45, 49

Bal, Mieke, 13
Banfield, Ann, 41
Barbauld, Anna Laetitia, 16–17, 21; and circle, 22

Beer, Gillian, 52, 56
Behn, Aphra: *Oroonoko*, 5
Bernal, Martin, 4, 110
Bhabha, Homi, 4, 11
Brantlinger, Patrick, 3, 113, 133n8
Bright, John, 115–16, 144n17
Brontë, Charlotte: *Jane Eyre*, 12, 24, 80, 84–94, 101; *Shirley*, 90; *Villette*, 86, 89, 139n11
Brontë, Emily: *Wuthering Heights*, 13
Brunton, Mary, 23
Bulwer-Lytton, Edward: *The Caxtons*, 53–54
Burney, Fanny, 6
Burton, Richard, 112
Butler, Josephine, 9
Butler, Marilyn, 21, 34
Byron, George Gordon, 37, 91, 96

Carlyle, Thomas, 3, 8, 11,
129*n*17; *Chartism,* 54–56
Carter, Paul, 35, 55, 57
Clarkson, Thomas, 22
Cobbett, William, 29–30, 45, 53
Cobden, Richard, 103, 116,
144*n*17
Collins, Wilkie: *The Moonstone,* 13,
113
Conant, Martha, 6, 91
Conrad, Joseph, 1, 3, 8, 122
Courtright, Paul, 92
Cowper, William, 23
Crosby, Alfred, 53

Dabydeen, David, 68–69, 132*n*17
Daniell, David, 128*n*5
Day, Thomas, 22–23, 30–32;
"The Dying Negro," 30,
132*n*13
Defoe, Daniel, 6, 134*n*19
DeQuincey, Thomas: *Confessions
of an English Opium Eater,* 110–
11, 114
DiBattista, Maria, 97–98
Dickens, Charles: *Bleak House,* 61,
77, 135*n*4; *David Copperfield,*
13, 52, 56; *Dombey and Son,* 12–
13, 51, 59–77; *Edwin Drood,*
12–13, 51, 74, 103–22; *Great
Expectations,* 13, 52, 76; *Little
Dorrit,* 63; *Martin Chuzzlewit,* 63
Disraeli, Benjamin, 54, 109,
134*n*14, 136*n*17
Doyle, Arthur Conan, 1
DuPlessis, Rachel, ix, 10, 129*n*14
Dykes, Eva, 17, 22

Eagleton, Terry, 1
East India Company, 37, 64
Edgeworth, Maria, 4, 6; *The Absentee,* 15, 33, 36; *Belinda,* 12,
15–34, 121; *Castle Rackrent* 15,

32, 36; *The Grateful Negro,* 20,
33
Edwards, Bryan, 32
Eliot, George: *Adam Bede,* 13, 56
Exeter Hall, 61, 116, 135*n*3
Eyre case, 116–17, 143*n*16

Fanon, Frantz, 95
Fay, Eliza, 140*n*15
Fielding, Henry, 6
Fielding, K. J., 115
Figueira, Dorothy, 91
Forster, E. M., 1, 95
Foucault, Michel, 7
Free Trade, 60–61, 66–67
Fryer, Peter, 30, 132*n*12

Gallagher, Catherine, 30
Gaskell, Elizabeth: *Cranford,* 63;
Mary Barton, 52–56, 74; *North
and South,* 13, 41, 46–51, 74
Gilbert, Sandra, 20, 82
Gilman, Sander, 99, 141*n*27
Goldsmith, Oliver, 6, 37
Green, Martin, 4–5, 8
Gubar, Susan, 20, 82

Haggard, Rider, 1
Harem, the, in English Litera-
ture, 94–95
Hennessy, Rosemary, x
Henty, G. A., 1
Hottentot, 141*n*27; "Hottentot
Venus," 99
Howe, Susanne, 6–7
Hulme, Peter, 3, 128*n*7, 139*n*12
Hurst, Michael, 33

James, C. L. R., 22, 132*n*12
James, Henry, 122
Jameson, Frederic, 133*n*7
Johnson, Samuel, 15, 23, 34, 37,
131*n*26
Joshi, Rama, 84

Kiernan, V. G., 4, 96, 109
Kingsley, Charles: *Alton Locke*, 52, 54, 56; *Westward Ho!*, 74
Kipling, Rudyard, xi, 1
Kirkham, Margaret, 19, 21, 42

Lawrence, T. E., 112
Lewis, Bernard, 124–25
Lewis, Matthew, 37
Liddle, Joanna, 84

Macherey, Pierre, 7, 32
Mani, Lata, 92
Mansfield Judgment, 42
Marryat, Capt. Frederick, 73–74, 134*n*13
Martineau, Harriet, 16, 66, 130*n*2
Marx, Karl, 100, 135*n*7
Maturin, Charles, 37
Meredith, George: *The Egoist*, 9
Meyer, Susan, 80–81, 138*n*3
Migration, 12, 53–57; *see also* Transportation
Mill, James, 33, 38–39, 91, 133*n*6
Mill, John Stuart, 116, 144*n*18
Milton, John, 21, 79
Mitchell, Thomas L., 57
Mohan, Rajeswari, x
Moore, Thomas: *Lalla Rookh*, 37
More, Hannah, 21, 23, 132*n*10
Mukherjee, Ramkrishna, 64, 136*n*10
Musselwhite, David, 64, 100, 133*n*9

Nandy, Ashis, 118–19, 140*n*16
National Tale, the, 6, 36–37
Nerlich, Michael, 63–64, 136*n*9
Newton, Judith, 60, 65
Niger Expedition, 59–60, 77

Opium, 108–11; opium trade, 12; Opium Wars, 67
Oriental Tale, the, 6, 37, 91, 128*n*9

Owenson, Sydney: *The Wild Irish Girl*, 36

Parks, Fanny, 84, 96, 119
Parry, Benita, 12, 128*n*10
Poovey, Mary, 128*n*11
Porter, Jane, 36
Purchas, Samuel, 37–38

Radcliffe, Anne, 21, 37
Raskin, Jonah, 2–3
Rhys, Jean, 139*n*7
Rich, Adrienne, 85
Richardson, Samuel, 6
Richon, Olivier, 94
Rousseau, Jean-Jacques, 31–32, 79, 131*n*23
Ruskin, John, 109

Said, Edward, 4–5, 7, 11, 57
Saint-Pierre, Jacques-Henri, 32
Sati, 12, 82, 84, 88–94, 139*n*9, 140*n*16
Schipper, Mineke, 13
Schreiner, Olive, 1, 9, 122, 129*n*13
Scott, Walter, 6, 36, 91, 96; *The Heart of Midlothian*, 24, 40
Sedgwick, Eve, 9, 107, 112
Seeley, J. R., 1
Semmel, Bernard, 60
Sharma, Arvind, 91–92
Showalter, Elaine, 93
Sleeman, W. H., 112, 120
Smollett, Tobias George, 6
Sonnerat, Pierre, 91
Southey, Robert, 23, 37; *The Curse of Kehama*, 91
Spencer, Herbert, 131*n*19
Spenser, Edmund, 5
Spivak, Gayatri, 4, 9, 80, 83, 85, 92
Steele, Richard, 6
Stein, Dorothy, 90

Stephen, James, 133n5
Sterne, Laurence, 6, 23, 128n8
Stocking, George, 8, 26, 33
Stokes, Eric, 48
Sypher, Wylie, 21–23, 33

Taylor, Meadows, 113
Temperley, Howard, 33
Thackeray, William, 99; *Cornhill to Grand Cairo*, 96; *Pendennis*, 76; *The Newcomes*, 62–64, 67, 73, 75–76, 81; *Vanity Fair*, 81, 83, 90, 94–102
"Thuggee," 12, 112–13, 120, 143n12, 144n20
Transportation, 12, 76–77, 138n27; *see also* Migration
Trevelyan, Charles, 120
Trevelyan, George Otto, 109, 142n7
Trollope, Anthony, 13

Viswanathan, Gauri, 4
Voltaire, 23, 91
Von Gunderrode, Karoline, 91

Wakefield, Edward Gibbon, 53
Weissman, Judith, 45
White, Hayden, 138n5
Wikkramasinha, Lakdasa, 123, 125
Wilberforce, William, 21
Wilde, Oscar: *The Picture of Dorian Gray*, 121
Williams, Eric, 60, 132n12
Williams, Raymond, 52, 68, 72, 123–25, 129n17, 134n15–16
Wilson, Angus, 121
Wilson, Edmund, 113, 120
Wollstonecraft, Mary, 18, 21–22, 32, 34, 79
Woolf, Leonard, ix
Woolf, Virginia, 8–9, 128n12